ICONS of

MUSCLE

SHOALS

An Introduction to American

Soul and R&B: Vol 3

D1699485

Kevin Tomlin

Cover based on a design by 40k Designs - www.fortyk.com

Illustrations: Photos Wikimedia Commons

Album Cover Images courtesy of Ace Records UK

Photo of Farfisa Organ courtesy of audiofanzine.com

Contents

Acknowledgements

I certainly give God thanks for giving me the inner strength to keep going by faith and keeping me in good health, as I work to complete each volume in this series. I am deeply grateful for the prayers and counsel of my Aunty Elsie since I was a child.

I must also thank my dear cousin Joanne Grey and my dear sister Denise for their deep wisdom and guidance during some difficult challenges in my life.

It has been a great pleasure to talk with the dynamic and powerful industry insider Charmain Elliott, who has shared with me her life's journey in the music industry, especially her views on the late Aretha Franklin, a key influence in her career, who is featured in this book.

I am profoundly grateful for the support I have received from Bill Spicer and for the work he has done to get the book ready for publication.

My thanks also go to Delroy Henry, Alfred Allen, Roger Moore, Elliott Browne, Juliet Fletcher, Lawrence Johnson and Ruben King, for all their encouragement, insights and support.

A final thank you goes to Neil Scaplehorn at Ace Records for permission to use the company's album cover images, and to Arnaud at audiofanzine.com for permission to use the image of the Farfisa portable organ.

Preface

I have been studying music of black origin for over thirty years, especially music from America's inner-cities and urban areas such as New Orleans, Chicago, Memphis, Muscle Shoals, Detroit, and Philadelphia. I have explored the origins of the distinctive sounds that have emerged from each location, and I have identified the key individuals who helped to create and define these sounds. This book and the others in the collection have been written to help lovers of Soul and R&B to understand where the music came from and who was responsible for its creation. *Icons of Muscle Shoals* tells the story not just of the headline names, such as Aretha Franklin and Wilson Pickett, but also of the lesser-known artists, who were often just as talented but lacked that stroke of luck that would have made them stars.

The story is based on the output from three recording studios that were set up within a few miles of each other in the Shoals. The singers who came to the studios are the stars of the story, of course, but the important part played by the musicians who formed the session bands, the songwriters, the producers and the sound engineers is also noted.

The Quad Cities make up a small urban area in North Alabama. It is an unlikely place for a musical explosion, but it became a place of pilgrimage for some of the greatest R&B performers of the sixties and seventies, and for many other artists from a variety of genres. The output of the three studios between 1961 and 1975 stands comparison with Stax and Chess in its contribution to the development of Soul and R&B music in the United States.

Above all, this story is a tribute to Rick Hall, the founding father and key musical architect of the Muscle Shoals signature sound.

1
INTRODUCTION: MUSCLE SHOALS

Muscle Shoals was a city with a population of approximately 6,000 people in the 1960s, where blacks and whites lived uneasily together during the period of racial segregation in the cotton belt of rural Alabama. The town is located on the south bank of the Tennessee River, alongside Sheffield and Tuscumbia. On the north bank of the river, opposite Muscle Shoals, stands Florence (the music of Muscle Shoals comes from Florence and Sheffield). Together the four towns make up the Quad Cities. The whole area is known as The Shoals.

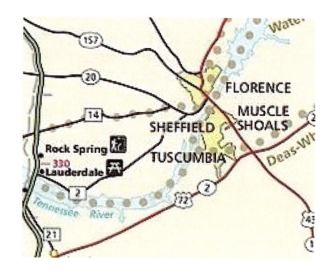

Muscle Shoals

Map: National Parks (Wikimedia Commons)

The city of Muscle Shoals was founded in 1923, on land where once the Cherokee people hunted. They gave the Tennessee River a beautiful name, that was a forecast of things to come. They called it the singing river.

The origin of the name Muscle Shoals is not clear, but it may well be a reference to the location on the river, where the water was shallow and mussels could be collected. To the south was an area where cotton grew well, and this was the basis of its early development. By the 1960s there was also one big industrial site, Reynolds Aluminium Corporation, which provided many local jobs.

The wider area was also becoming well-known within the music industry. Picture in your mind a triangle shape, formed by Memphis at one corner, with Nashville on another, and Muscle Shoals on the third. The Soul of Memphis met the Country music of Nashville in this sleepy corner of northern Alabama, and the sound of Muscle Shoals was born. The fusion of R&B, Country and Soul that emerged from the studios in The Shoals completed the third element of a powerful and dynamic trio. The music that was created here could not be duplicated on the East or West coast in any form whatsoever!

Sam Phillips, who founded Sun Records in Memphis, was born in The Shoals. He worked for a while at a local radio station WLAY (AM), which played a mixture of "white" and "black" music and pointed the way for the two styles to cross-pollinate. Local black singers such as Arthur Alexander and James Carr were influenced by the Country music from Nashville, while white musicians were able to incorporate elements of Blues and Gospel into their work.

Florence, just across the river from Muscle Shoals, was the birthplace of W.C. Handy, who formalised the songs that he heard on the cotton plantations. The town is often referred to as the "birthplace of the Blues", as a result. In honour of Handy, an annual festival takes place in The Shoals every year, featuring Blues, Jazz, Gospel, R&B, Rock and Country music. The W. C. Handy Music Festival is a fitting tribute not just to him but also to all the singers, musicians and technicians who put Muscle Shoals on the music map.

Like a lot of American tales, the story starts with a dream. Rick Hall met Sam Phillips and decided to follow in his footsteps, dreaming of becoming a successful songwriter and record producer. Who knows, he could even set up a recording studio and a record label!

The Old Railway Bridge at Muscle Shoals, now a walkway

Photo: Carol M. Highsmith 2010 (Wikimedia Commons)

2

RICK HALL: THE BIRTH OF FAME

Roe Erister Hall was born in 1932. His family were sharecroppers in Forest Grove, Mississippi. He acquired a nickname, Rick. His mother left home when he was only four years old. He grew up with his grandparents, father and sister in Franklin County, Alabama, where Hall learned to play guitar. Later, during his military service, he played in a band and started thinking about a career in music.

After his stint in the army, he took a job in Florence at Reynolds Aluminum. He married in 1955, but within eighteen months, his wife Faye died in a car crash. This tragedy was compounded by the death of his father just two weeks later in a farm accident. Hall sought solace in alcohol and went through some tough times. He also joined a local music group called Carmol Taylor and the Country Pals, playing guitar, mandolin and fiddle, touring the local area and playing on a weekly radio show on WERH in Hamilton. As he recovered from the dual tragedies of 1957, he set up a new group with Billy Sherrill and Dan Penn, which they named the Fairlanes. It was during this time that Hall started writing songs, with some success. Roy Orbison, George Jones and Brenda Lee all recorded songs that he had written during the late 1950s.

In 1959 Tom Stafford offered to form a music publishing company with Rick Hall and Billy Sherrill, which they called FAME, Florence Alabama Music Enterprises. It operated out of one of the rooms above a pharmacy in Florence, which was owned by Stafford's father. Tom had set up a small recording facility there, which he called SPAR, Stafford Publishing and Recording. He had also formed a song-writing partnership with a young singer called Arthur Alexander. They all worked out of the same building. Many of the young musicians who were later to help establish FAME Studios came to SPAR.

Suddenly, in 1960, Hall was left with nothing, when his two partners dissolved the partnership, possibly because they found Hall too demanding. Fortunately, he decided to carry on without them. He paid a dollar to keep the FAME name, borrowed some money and set up a studio in an old tobacco warehouse on Wilson Dam Road in Muscle Shoals in 1961, which he called FAME studio. Sherrill left the partnership soon after Hall, as he was offered a job at Sam Phillips' new studio in Nashville. He went on to work with some of Country music's top names, including George Jones and Tammy Wynette.

Meanwhile, one of Rick Hall's first recordings in the Wilson Dam Road studio was a song called "You Better Move On", which he recorded with that young black singer from SPAR Studio, Arthur Alexander. Hall took the tape to Nashville and tried to find a record company interested in leasing the recording. After a number of rejections, Noel Ball signed a deal at Dot Records. Ball took not just the recording but Alexander too! Hall watched as the single went on to achieve gold record status. Hall had signed a contract that gave him just 2% of sales income from the song, but it sold well enough to subsidise the building of a new studio in Avalon Road, for which Hall retained the FAME name.

Hall sought advice from Owen Bradley, a producer from Nashville, in the design of the new facility. The building was twenty feet by seventy feet, with just one studio space. Bradley added echo chambers, which were a key element of the studio's rich sound.

Rick Hall in the FAME Studio 2014

Photo: Carol M. Highsmith (Wikimedia Commons)

The session musicians that Hall had brought together at SPAR and at the Wilson Dam Road studio included members of a band called Dan Penn and the Pallbearers, who travelled around in a hearse. Jerry Carrigan, Norbert Putnam and David Briggs were young, but they had style! Together with Earl "Peanutt" Montgomery, Spooner Oldham and Terry Thompson, they now became the first session men at Avalon Road and started to build a reputation that was later to bring a string of big names to Muscle Shoals.

Norbert Putnam has spoken about the music that they wanted to play: "Our entire orientation was R&B. We were strictly young kids who loved soul music." The simple set-up in the studio suited the song, with open-miked recording and low amplification.

In several ways, Hall's story echoes that of Jim Stewart at Stax Records. Like Stewart, Hall grew up in an environment where Country music was dominant. Both these men were, however, attracted to music of black origin and opened the doors of their studios to everyone. It was a surprising thing to do, especially in the southern states where segregation was deeply embedded. Hall has explained the importance of this decision: "Black music helped broaden my musical horizons and open my eyes and ears to the widespread appeal of the so-called 'race' music that later became known as 'Rhythm and Blues'.

He was fortunate to find in Dan Penn and the Pallbearers a group of young session musicians who had the ability to deliver the sound that he was striving for and a budding songwriter, who would go on to write hundreds of songs

FAME Recording Studios 2010

Photo: Carol M. Highsmith Library of Congress (Wikimedia Commons)

3

FAME: THE EARLY YEARS

Rick Hall's first problem was to attract business to the FAME studios. One young singer was already "in the building", of course, Arthur Alexander. That was easy. But there weren't many experienced performers in the Muscle Shoals area that he could bring in. To solve the problem, he looked to Nashville and Atlanta, which were already important centres for popular music production. Hall made contact with a number of agents and producers, including Bill Lowery, Felton Jarvis, and Buddy Killen. As a result, Tommy Roe, Joe Tex and the Tams came to Muscle Shoals to record. Hall also auditioned a number of local singers, amongst whom Jimmy Hughes stood out. These were the artists who helped put FAME on the musical map.

Arthur Alexander

Arthur Alexander was born in Sheffield, one of the quad cities, in 1940. He joined a Gospel group, the Heartstrings, whilst still at high school and recorded his first single in 1960. It was a song that he had co-written with Tom Stafford, called "Sally Sue Brown", which was released by Judd Records under the name June Alexander (June was short for Junior). It is a blues tune, probably inspired by Alexander's father, who played bottleneck style blues guitar. It is a good song, but not original enough to make any impact.

The song that turned FAME's fortunes in 1961 was very different, a slow Country-influenced Soul song. "You Better Move On" is a classic. In the UK it was covered by the Rolling Stones and the Hollies, and the Beatles took notice too. They covered Alexander's 1962 release "Anna (Go To Him)" and also included two of his songs in their early live performances: "Soldier of Love" and "A Shot of Rhythm & Blues".

In 1963, Steve Alaimo recorded another of Alexander's songs, "Every Day I Have To Cry", which entered the top fifty on both the Billboard and Cash Box charts. In the UK the song was recorded by Dusty Springfield and released in 1964.

Arthur Alexander is remembered largely for the songs that he wrote. He died in 1993, just after completing a come-back album entitled "Lonely Just Like Me" (Elektra/Nonesuch), which is a quiet, understated set of songs, that is a fitting tribute to him as a performer.

Jason Ankeny (music critic for AllMusic) has called Alexander a "country-soul pioneer", describing his music as "the stuff of genius, a poignant and deeply intimate body of work...". It is possible that, without him, much of what Rick Hall achieved at Muscle Shoals might not have happened.

Recommended Track:

1961 Arthur Alexander: "You'd Better Move On"

Jimmy Hughes

Jimmy Hughes was born in 1938 and grew up in Leighton, not far from Muscle Shoals. His early experience of performing came at high school, when he became a member of the Singing Clouds Gospel quartet, in 1956. In 1962, he was introduced to Rick Hall by a friend, Bob Carl Bailey, who had also sung in the Singing Clouds quartet.

Rick Hall gave Hughes an audition and then recorded him singing a Hall/Ivy song called "I'm Qualified". It was released on the Guyden label, a Philadelphia company, but failed to make an impression. Hughes started singing secular songs, performing in local clubs and building up his experience. He also started writing songs, one of which he took with him on his next visit to FAME in 1964. "Steal Away" was based on a

Gospel song and suited Hughes' style. It was to prove an important song in the development of Muscle Shoals sound.

"Steal Away" was the first hit recorded at the new FAME studio and set the pattern for future success. It was a powerful ballad, which had been recorded in one take, with the FAME session band, with Jerry Carrigan on drums, Norbert Putnam on bass, David Briggs on keyboards and Terry Thompson on guitar. Thanks to the exposure that the song was given on radio stations in the southern states, it sold well, rising to number seventeen on the Billboard Hot 100.

The national success of Hughes' single enabled Rick Hall to sign a distribution deal with Vee-Jay Records for his FAME releases. That was an important step, as it meant that Hall did not have to hawk each recording he made around a multitude of agents and record companies, until he found a deal.

Jimmy Hughes cut four more singles at FAME that made the charts between 1964 and 1967. He also recorded an album called "Steal Away" that was released by Vee-Jay, which featured several songs written by Dan Penn and Spooner Oldham, working together for the first time. He then moved to Stax Records in Memphis, where his first single, "I Like Everything About You" (1968), issued on the Volt label, went to number twenty-one on the R&B chart. Subsequent songs failed to chart, however, and Hughes retired from the music industry in 1970.

Three albums of Hughes' songs have been released on Kent Records, two are collections of the FAME recordings and the third is a compilation of the songs recorded at Stax.

The importance of Hughes' early success was that it established FAME as a recording centre in the R&B/Soul music field. It gave credibility to the white musicians who played on the sessions and to Rick Hall too, who produced all the tracks. Hughes, a cousin of Percy Sledge, became a prototype for later artists in Muscle Shoals and even for Johnnie Tayor and Al Green in Memphis.

Jimmy Hughes 1967

Photo: Atco Records Trade Ad (Wikimedia Commons)

Recommended Track:

1964 Jimmy Hughes: "Steal Away"

The Tams

The Tams were a group of five black singers from Atlanta, Georgia, who came together in 1960. They chose the group's name as a reference to the Tam O'Shanter hats that they wore on stage. The founding members were Joseph Pope, Robert Lee Smith, Horace Key, Charles Pope and Floyd Ashton. They had their first hit in 1962, when they recorded a Joe South song called "Untie Me", but 1964 saw them reach the number one spot on the Billboard and Cash Box R&B charts. The song, "What Kind of Fool (Do You Think I Am)", released on ABC-Paramount, also reached number nine on the Pop chart. They recorded the single at the FAME studios with Rick Hall and the FAME session band, Norbert Putnam (bass), David Briggs (piano), Jerry Carrigan (drums), Terry

Thompson and Earl "Peanutt" Montgomery (guitars), with Jill Shires on flute.

The song was written by Ray Whitley, who wrote many of the Tams' songs, including their next big hit "Hey Girl Don't Bother Me". The single was released in 1964, charting at number forty-one on the Billboard Hot 100 Singles chart and number ten on the Billboard Best-Selling Soul Singles chart. In 1971 the re-issued song went to number one on the UK Official Pop Singles Chart on 18th September (three weeks) and also on the Irish Singles Chart on 30th September (one week), becoming extremely popular on the Northern Soul circuit in England. The Tams appeared on the BBC TV show *Top of the Pops* eight times in 1971!

Recommended Tracks:

1964 The Tams: "What Kind of Fool (Do You Think I Am)"

Joe Tex

Joe Tex was born Joseph Arrington Jr. in 1935 in Rogers, Texas. He played baritone saxophone at high school and sang in the choir of his local Pentecostal church. After winning several talent contests, he was signed first to King Records in 1955 and then Ace Records in 1958. In 1960 he moved to Anna Records in Detroit and then on to Dial Records. The frequent changes are an indication that his single releases weren't making much impression on the market.

He was, however, becoming increasingly popular as a live act, opening for a series of big names, including Jackie Wilson, James Brown and Little Richard. Then, in 1964, his luck finally changed. He came to Muscle Shoals to record "Hold What You've Got" with Rick Hall at FAME, and, after thirty songs that failed to chart, the thirty-first reached number five on the Billboard Hot 100. It went to number one on the R&B chart, remaining on the chart for eleven weeks and achieving gold certification in 1966.

Joe Tex 1965

Photo: Dial Records Trade Ad (Wikimedia Commons)

The second number one record of his career was "I Want To (Do Everything For You)" on the Billboard Hot Rhythm & Blues Singles Chart week-ending 9th October 1965 (3 weeks) followed by "A Sweet Woman Like You" week-ending 8th January 1966 (1 week).

Joe Tex went on to have three more million-selling hits with "Skinny Legs and All" in 1967, "I Gotcha" in 1972 and "Ain't Gonna Bump No More (With No Big Fat Woman)" in 1977. During the mid-sixties, he achieved a new higher level of consistency, with six R&B charting songs in 1965 (two number ones on the Billboard Singles chart listing), five top-forty R&B singles in 1966, and that second million-seller in 1967.

For nine years he had struggled to find a hit song. As soon as he came to FAME, everything seemed to click.

Recommended Tracks:

1964 Joe Tex: "Hold What You've Got"

1965 Joe Tex: "I Want To (Do Everything For You)"

Joe Simon came from California to FAME Recording Studio in 1965 to record with Rick Hall. He cut the song "Let's Do It Over", which took him onto the Billboard R&B chart for the first time, when the song was released on the Vee-Jay label. The single reached number thirteen, setting Simon on the road to greater success touring and recording.

Recommended Track:

1965 Joe Simon: "Let's Do It Over"

4

FAME: THE SONGWRITERS

Dan Penn

Wallace Daniel Pennington was born in a small farming community called Molloy in 1941. In 1957 his family moved to Vernon, Alabama, near Muscle Shoals, where Penn joined a band (Benny Cagle and the Rhythm Swingers). This gave him the opportunity to play sing some of the songs that he had started writing, including "Is a Bluebird Blue?", which was picked up by Conway Twitty, who released his version in 1959. Penn later joined the Mark V band, before forming Dan Penn & the Pallbearers.

He also began working as a songwriter at the SPAR studio, where he met Rick Hall. One of the first things that Hall did when he built his new studio was to offer Penn a job. Hall clearly understood that in popular music, everything starts with the song. Penn has spoken about taking up the offer: "Rick Hall built himself a studio, Fame, and wanted me to write for him. He was good enough to pay me 25 bucks a week, so I started writing for him in '63 and moved to Muscle Shoals from my hometown in Vernon, Alabama". (See John Pidgeon's article in the Online Library of Music Journalism, 1991). Carrigan, Briggs, Montgomery and Putnam were quickly brought on board too, as FAME's first session band.

Penn had grown up listening to a wide range of music. He was comfortable with a variety of musical styles, and that was going to stand him in good stead in the years to come. One key element in his musical education had come through the radio broadcasts that he had heard on the Nashville station WLAC, which was playing spirituals and R&B for a Black audience. The impact of the music on him was considerable:

"My ears just told me what was good. That was the start of it". (Quoted on the Memphis Music Hall of Fame website).

In 1963 Penn was just happy to be involved with the music that he loved. His friends were in the studio with him, and Rick Hall was dreaming of making FAME famous. Penn involved himself in every aspect of work in the studio, acting as Hall's right-hand man. But by the end of 1964, the promise of 1963 seemed to be lost.

Carrigan, Briggs and Putnam decided to move to Nashville, where they felt they could find bigger and better opportunities and where they could earn more than the basic session rates that Rick Hall was paying them. Penn suddenly found himself doubting his future at FAME.

His decision was to abandon singing and playing guitar and to concentrate on songwriting. In addition, he set about building his technical skills and learning how to be an effective record producer: "That's what I'm gonna be, a studio cat" (Memphis Music Hall of Fame website). After the disappointment of his friends leaving, he needed to get things moving again, and he soon found the way. He had already crossed paths with Spooner Oldham, as they had met while playing in different local bands. Oldham had also worked for Rick Hall on various sessions, including overdubbing a Hammond organ part on to Arthur Alexander's "You Better Move On". Penn and Oldham started writing songs together, simply working ideas out on guitar and piano that they felt would suit the Soul and R&B market. Their first success came when Joe Simon recorded "Let's Do It Over" in 1965, with Rick Hall producing. The single was released on Vee-Jay Records, spending four months in the top twenty of the national charts.

From this small beginning, Penn and Oldham went on to establish themselves as major songwriters. Percy Sledge recorded "It Tears Me Up" and James and Bobby Purify picked up "I'm Your Puppet" in 1966. That same year, Penn was one of the writers of "You Left the Water Running", along with Rick Hall and Oscar Franck, which was recorded by Billy Young on the Chess label. The song was also set to be covered by Wilson Pickett. When Otis Redding came visiting FAME just before Pickett was due, Rick Hall asked Otis to record a demo of the song, to help with the set-up. Pickett made his recording soon after. Many years later, Otis' version appeared on 1987's "The Otis Redding Story".

A new session band was formed by Rick Hall and things looked good for Dan Penn. However, although the songwriting was going well, the other ambition of his was to produce records and, with Rick Hall firmly in the driving seat, that wasn't happening. Once more, Penn took a bold decision. He had started working for Press Publishing in Memphis in 1966 and had crossed paths with Chips Moman, the boss at American Sound Studio in that city. Now the chance came to work with Moman, songwriting and producing. Penn seized the chance.

Two Moman/Penn songs from 1967 are absolute classics, James Carr's "The Dark End of the Street" and Aretha Franklin's "Do Right Woman – Do Right Man". And finally in that same year, Penn produced his first hit single. The Box Tops came to American Sound Studio to record a Wayne Carson song "The Letter", with Penn entrusted with production duties. The single sold over a million copies and stayed at the top of the Billboard Hot 100 for four weeks. Dan Penn had made some very good decisions!

A few years later, Penn was able to leave American Sound and set up his own studio in Memphis which he called Beautiful Sounds. This gave him the opportunity to start performing again and in 1972 he recorded his debut album "Nobody's Fool", which features a couple of tracks written by

Penn with Spooner Oldham, "Ain't No Love" and "Raining in Memphis".

Twenty years later, Penn released a solo album called "Do Right Man", which highlights songs that he wrote at Muscle Shoals with Spooner Oldham and then went on to release a live album "Moments From This Theatre" with Oldham in 1998. In the new century, Penn moved to Nashville, where he set up another studio and formed a record label (Dandy Records). Three more albums have been released: "Blue Nite Lounge" (2001), "Junkyard Junkie" (2008) and "The Fame Recordings" (2012), the last of which features twenty-three previously unreleased songs from the years in Muscle Shoals. Fittingly, he was inducted into the Alabama Music Hall of Fame in 2013.

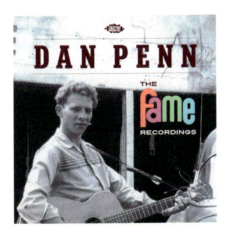

Dan Penn's 2012 album on Kent Records

(Used with permission of Ace Records UK)

Spooner Oldham

Dewey Lindon Oldham Jr. was born in Center Star, Alabama, in 1943. His father played mandolin and encouraged Dewey to take an interest in music. The nickname "Spooner" came as a cruel reference to an accident he had as a child, in which he lost the sight in his right eye. He was hit by a spoon.

Dewey played in bands at school and enrolled at North Alabama University on leaving high school. He was attracted, however, to a career in music and soon left to find work at local recording studios, playing piano and organ. He had joined a band called Hollis Dixon and the Keynotes, that played in the Muscle Shoals area and may well have crossed paths with Dan Penn, who was playing in a different band working in the same area. They possibly met at SPAR Studio, above the drugstore, which they both visited, and they certainly met at FAME Studios, where they soon started writing songs together.

The songwriting duo produced around four hundred songs over the years, many of which became national hits. Many of them are referenced in other chapters of this book. When Penn moved to American Sound Studio in 1967, Oldham stayed on in Muscle Shoals until a replacement keyboard player could be hired and then followed Penn to Memphis.

Together, they produced a string of hits for the Box Tops, the Sweet Inspirations and many other artists. The session playing also brought Oldham a host of opportunities to play with some big names in the industry. His smooth, spectral organ sound can be heard on a series of hits, first at FAME and Norala Studios, and then at American Sound in Memphis.

As the impact of Southern Soul grew weaker, especially after the assassination of Dr. Martin Luther King, Oldham moved on to Los Angeles and widened the scope of his playing. He worked with Linda Ronstadt, Gene Clark, Neil Young and Bob Dylan, sometimes in the studio but also on the road.

In 1993, Oldham joined a group of musicians from the old times to play on Arthur Alexander's album "Lonely Just Like Me".

In 1998 Penn and Oldham teamed up again, this time as performers! They completed a tour of the UK, which resulted in the issue of a live album entitled "Moments From This Theatre".

In 2015, a company called Light In The Attic reissued Oldham's solo album from the seventies, "Pot Luck". It is a great way to remember his talent. In recognition of his contribution to popular music, he has been inducted into the Musicians Hall of Fame, the Rock and Roll Hall of Fame (2009), and the Alabama Music Hall of Fame (2014).

"When we first sat down and started writing, we liked each other, and that's a good start," says Penn. "But after night after night of writing, this chemistry kept building. Now if we sit down to write or play, we can almost read each other's mail, we've done it so much. When we play, that's as close to the '60s as you can get, when we were at the Fame studios, because there'd be nobody there but us."

(Quoted from *No Depression*, the online roots music magazine)

Donnie Fritts

Donnie Fritts was born in Florence, Alabama, not far from the location of the FAME studios, in 1942. His interest in music as a teenager developed quickly; by the age of fifteen he was playing drums or keyboards in local bands, including Hollis Dixon & the Keynotes. This was the band that Spooner Oldham played with.

Fritts was also a songwriter. By the late fifties, he had written songs with Spooner Oldham and Dann Penn. He met Arthur Alexander in 1958, possibly at the SPAR Studio, and they became great friends, writing songs together. Some of the songs he co-wrote were later recorded by Tommy Roe, Percy Sledge, Dusty Springfield and the Box Tops.

Fritts was involved in many of the early recordings at FAME, working alongside Briggs, Carrigan and Putnam.

In 1965 he signed a contract with a Nashville publishing company and went on to build his career there. He was invited to play keyboards for Kris Kristofferson and was a member of his band for many years.

Fritts recorded a solo album in 1974 called "Prone to Lean" at Muscle Shoals Sound Studio, with production duties shared by Kris Kristofferson and Jerry Wexler. A second album appeared in 1997 entitled "Everybody's Got a Song", with a string of guests including Dan Penn and Spooner Oldham. A third album "One Foot in the Groove" was released in 2008, produced by Dan Penn and Ron Laury in Nashville. "Oh My Goodness" was released in 2015. They are all interesting albums, but with a strong Nashville influence.

Thanks to his contact with Kris Kristofferson, Fritts also appeared in five films, including three made by Sam Peckinpah.

Donnie Fritts was inducted into the Alabama Music Hall of Fame in 2008. He died in Alabama in 2019.

Just before his death, Fritts had released one last album. "June" (2018) is a tribute to his old friend Arthur Alexander, recorded at Muscle Shoals Sound Studio, with David Hood (bass) amongst the band members. His voice is not strong, but the sincerity is clear. The track listing is a wonderful set of Alexander's songs, all written by various combinations of Alexander, Fritts and Penn, introduced by the title track, a personal memory by Fritts.

In an article on *The Bitter Southerner* website, Chuck Reece reports Donnie's comments about his friend: "We became very close friends. The year was 1958. Black and white folks didn't mix very much back then. We did. It was never an issue for us. Never."

5

FAME: THE FIRST SESSION BAND

Any studio is only as good as its session players. At FAME there were a group of young white men, who all liked the R&B music that they heard on local radio stations. Several of these musicians had played together in bands in the Shoals area and knew other well.

Norbert Putnam

Norbert Auvin Putnam was born in 1942. He grew up near Florence, learning to play an upright bass. In his teens he joined David Briggs and Jerry Carrigan in a local group. They were all too young to drive, so Garrigan's father usually provided a "taxi" service to get them to wherever they were performing.

They were spotted by Tom Stafford, who hired them to work at the SPAR studio, above the Florence drugstore, where they met Rick Hall and Billy Sherrill. The boys' main task was to record demo versions of the songs that the owners were writing, which could then be used to sell the songs to singers who were looking for original material to record.

When Rick Hall found himself suddenly pushed out of SPAR, he set about establishing FAME, which he wanted to make bigger and better than the previous venture. He hired the boys, plus several of their friends, to work at the new studios, not just record demos of new songs but also to provide a backing band for the singers that he hoped to attract. It is not hard to imagine the excitement these teenagers felt when they played on the recording of "You Better Move On" and watched the single go to number twenty-four on the Billboard Hot 100 in March 1962.

Arthur Alexander's hit was followed by more successes for Tommy Roe, Jimmy Hughes, the Tams and Joe Tex. Then, in 1965, the three friends decided to move on. The money on offer in Nashville, only 125 miles away, was tempting, and so was the opportunity to play with some of the industry's top names.

Norbert Putnam 2014

Photo: Composemusic (Wikimedia Commons)

Norbert Putnam was soon playing for Elvis Presley, Roy Orbison, Linda Ronstadt and many more well-known singers. He also got involved in producing, specializing in working with non-country singers who came to record in Nashville. He joined Area Code 615, an eight-man supergroup, and opened Quadrafonic Studio in 1970, along with David Briggs. One of his strengths was his ability to play acoustic bass, an echo of those early-teen years at home in Alabama.

Putnam was inducted into the Musicians Hall of Fame in 2019.

David Briggs

David Briggs was born in 1943 in Killen, Alabama. He played keyboards on his first recording session at the age of fourteen for James Joiner at Tune Records. He then worked in the Shoals area with Putnam, Carrigan, and Terry Thompson. In 1962 he signed for Decca Records and found himself travelling frequently to Nashville.

In 1964, he moved there and found that his versatility meant that he was never short of session work. He was also offered the chance to play as part of a touring band for Tommy Roe, who had come to Muscle Shoals in those early years of FAME. He was backing Tommy Roe on stage in Washington D.C. in 1964, when the Beatles made their first concert appearance in the United States. (More about that later).

He recorded with Elvis Presley, Joan Baez, B.B. King, Tony Joe White and many more singers, across a wide variety of genres.

As we seen, he opened a studio with Norbert Putnam. When that closed in 1976, he opened his own House of David. Like Putnam, he was a member of Area Code 615. When he had some spare time, he recorded a string of commercials for some of America's biggest corporations.

David Briggs was inducted into the Alabama Music Hall of Fame in 1999, and into the Musicians Hall of Fame in 2019.

Jerry Carrigan

Jerry Kirby Carrigan was born in 1943 in Florence, Alabama, in the Shoals. His father bought him a drum kit when he quite young and encouraged him to play. The first band that Jerry played in was Little Joe Allen and the Offbeats; they liked to learn the R&B songs that heard on the radio.

Jerry's father was confident that his son could earn money from playing the drums and so he set about finding some other local lads to form a group, that could play at student parties. The two lads who were invited to join were David Briggs and Norbert Putnam. Mr. Carrigan had a good eye for talent! The band was named the Mark V and Mr. Carrigan was their booking agent and their taxi driver.

It wasn't long before the boys found their way to SPAR Studio, where they met Tom Stafford, Billy Sherrill and, of course, Rick Hall. They started working there, recording demos of songs that the owners and other visitors were writing, and so met Dan Penn, Spooner Oldham, Donnie Fritts and Terry Thompson. Dan Penn started singing with the Mark V, which became Dan Penn & the Pallbearers.

When Rick Hall's venture with Sherrill and Stafford was terminated, Jerry Carrigan and his friends were given the opportunity to go the FAME. It is not hard to see the attraction of working in a recording studio, not just making demo tapes but also backing professional singers. All the SPAR musicians and songwriters came to work at the new studio. Within a few weeks, Arthur Alexander had brought a big smile to their faces with his first hit. That was followed, as we have seen, by a series of successful recordings in the early sixties.

The next significant event for Carrigan and the others occurred early in 1964, when Tommy Roe came back to record at FAME. Roe had just been booked, along with the Righteous Brothers and several other acts, to open for the Beatles at their first concert in the States, and Roe needed a backing band. He asked the boys to be that band. In February, they boarded a plane for Washington D.C. and they took part in that historic concert. Not bad for a trio of young lads from the Shoals! Unsurprisingly, it wasn't long before they decided to leave Rick Hall's FAME Studios and move to Nashville.

Carrigan played a session man in Nashville for over thirty

years. He developed a style of drumming that suited Nashville's Country music, but his playing retained an element of that Soul and R&B that he had grown up listening to and which he brought to songs recorded at FAME.

Jerry Carrigan was inducted into the Alabama Music Hall of Fame in 2010, and then into the Musicians Hall of Fame in 2019, the year of his death.

Rick Hall has described what made Jerry Carrigan special, in *The Man From Muscle Shoals*:

"Jerry was the first drummer I ever knew who could synchronize his kick and snare drum while simultaneously playing the open and closed sock cymbal".

Carrigan himself is quoted on the Alabama Music Hall of Fame website, describing his sound:

"I started playing real loose, deep-sounding snare drums on country records. Billy Sherrill loved it. So, I started experimenting with different things, different kinds of drums. I bought the first set of concert tom-toms that were in Nashville. I think that's one reason the producers liked my sound. I had a different approach."

Carrigan certainly played a key role in making Nashville the "Music City" that it is today.

Earl "Peanutt" Montgomery

Omar Earl Montgomery was born into a sharecropping family from Iron City, Tennessee, in the 1941, but he grew up in Florence, Alabama. His father was a guitarist and fiddle player, who also gave singing lessons. He encouraged all his children to take an interest in music, which they did.

Earl started playing piano and guitar from the age of six. His sister Melba was a singer, who won a talent contest at the Grand Ole Opry with her brother Carl and went on to have a successful career in Nashville, singing Country music.

In 1961 Montgomery joined FAME and played on the early hits.

He liked black R&B music, but he was also a fan of Country. When he met later George Jones, he decided that he would go to Nashville, to write Country songs and play. The gamble paid off. George Jones recorded seventy-three of his songs! He also became one of the top session men in Music City and played bass as a staff member of the Grand Ole Opry. And he achieved all of that without being able to read music:

"I never did learn to write and read music. I only know an "f" note on a guitar, but I compiled a method of a song. I don't read charts and numbered charts like you find in a recording studio. But I can read what the beats are." (Interview with Peanutt Montgomery on *The Soul of the American Actor* website).

In 1997, he was awarded the Arthur Alexander Songwriter's Award by the Alabama Music Hall of Fame.

He and his wife have set up a museum and recording studio in Sheffield, Alabama, which is packed with memorabilia of Montgomery's life in music.

Terry Thompson

Terry Thompson was born in 1941. He was from Florence, where FAME was founded and was one of the regular visitors to Tom Stafford's SPAR Studio. He played guitar and wrote songs, including "A Shot of Rhythm and Blues", which became the B-side of Arthur Alexander's "You Better Move On". Thompson was a member of the Fairlanes, along with

Rick Hall and Billy Sherrill, so it is no surprise that he was signed up to work at the first FAME Studio in 1961.

He bought a Gretch guitar during that year that he used in the studio, backing many of the early artists who came to record with Rick Hall, including Jimmy Hughes, who had the first big hit record from the second FAME Studio. Sadly, just as Muscle Shoals music began to take off, Thompson died, in 1965. He was inducted into the Alabama Music Hall of Fame in 2010.

*

Dan Penn, Spooner Oldham and Donnie Fritts were all involved in many of the early sessions, as songwriters, musicians or assistant producers. Most of these young men from the local area, aged between eighteen and twenty, emerged from two groups, the Fairlanes and the Pallbearers. They all knew each other from their visits to SPAR Studio and they all knew Rick Hall. They were the people who helped Rick Hall build the reputation of FAME Recording Studios and that he came to depend on. It must have come as a serious shock, when some of them suddenly decided to leave.

Putnam, Briggs and Carrigan decided to move to Nashville, where the rates of pay for session work were higher and where they could possibly set up their own studios.

6

6
FAME: THE SECOND SESSION BAND

Rick Hall acted quickly to form a new session band. He recruited people that he knew, as before. The core of the new band were four very talented musicians: Jimmy Johnson, Roger Hawkins, Barry Beckett and David Hood. In addition, Spooner Oldham and Junior Lowe were frequently added to the group. Dan Penn was still providing major support for Rick Hall in the studio.

Jimmy Johnson

Jimmy Ray Johnson was born in 1943 in Sheffield, Alabama. He took up the guitar as a youngster and, at the age of fifteen, earned ten dollars playing at a sock hop. His parents liked Country music, but Jimmy was drawn to black R&B music when he heard Chuck Berry.

When Rick Hall opened FAME Studios in 1961, Johnson was one of the first people to apply for a job there. He was employed to do clerical work and then began helping out in the recording studio as a sound engineer.

He was still playing guitar, as a member of the Del-Rays, alongside Roger Hawkins on drums, Billy Cofield on saxophone, and Billy Scott on organ. The group were able to record a number of songs with Rick Hall producing, including "The Girl That Radiates That Charm" in 1962 on the FAME Records label, and "Fortune Teller" in 1965.

Johnson was an obvious choice to join the new studio session band that Rick Hall had to set up. He played on a couple of sessions in 1965, but things really took off in 1966, when FAME welcomed Arthur Conley, Percy Sledge, Clarence

Carter, Wilson Pickett and Aretha Franklin.

Johnson often played rhythm guitar on FAME sessions, with various lead guitarists being invited to augment the band when necessary.

Roger Hawkins

Roger Hawkins was born in 1945 in Mishawaka, Indiana. He grew up in a town called Greenhill in Alabama, around twenty miles from Muscle Shoals. At the age of thirteen, he started to play drums and soon joined the Del-Rays. They began recording at FAME Studios, where he met Rick Hall, who invited him to join the new session band. He also found work at Quin Ivy's Norala Studio, where one of his first sessions was Percy Sledge's "When a Man Loves a Woman". What a great start to his career as a session musician!

In any band, the drummer is the anchor. The beat they set is the heartbeat of the music. All the best studios had a great drummer, and FAME was no exception. Hawkins was a master of his art, despite not being able to read music. None of the band could! As Hawkins has explained, his skill was listening to a song and finding a drumbeat that enhanced it. He listened and stored musical ideas, ready to use them when the right song came along:

"I was a better listener than player and I think the other guys were too". (My Drum Lessons, Sunday, April 30th, 2017)

"...they loved music and they had catalogs of music in their brains, just like I had a catalog of stuff where I could pull out certain things and make it work with newer stuff." (Roger Hawkins speaking with Daniel Kreps, Rolling Stone magazine, May 2021)

There are many recordings that demonstrate his skills and his originality. For "I'll Take You There" he developed an intricate cymbal pattern with a soft edge, accompanied by David Hood on bass, who provided a funky bottom line. His solid back beats transformed such songs as "I Never Loved a Man (The Way I Love You)" or "Respect Yourself". The intro of "Respect Yourself" has drumbeats that move from soft to hard and back to soft, a reggae pattern influenced by sounds originally developed on the island of Jamaica.

The biggest influence on Hawkin's playing style was much nearer home: Al Jackson Jr. in Memphis. Hawkins has described the impact of hearing "Green Onions" for the first time and rushing out to buy the record. The music recorded at Stax Records provided him with some wonderful examples to follow.

However, Hawkins didn't just copy. He was also an experimenter. In an interview with Jeff Porter of Modern Drummer, Hawkins explained how he got the sound Paul Simon wanted for "Kodachrome":

"I call it a loping feel. That was the drums, but that didn't get the feel enough… And I sure as hell couldn't play it on the bass drum. So I got an old two-inch tape box, like the big reels used to come in. I put some newspaper in the box and played the pattern on it with hard vibes mallets. I listened back to it, though, and it wasn't quite cutting through. So I kept changing the packing in the box until it came through well. That's where the loping feel comes from. I don't know if that drum part would have sounded that good without it".

Barry Beckett

Barry Edward Beckett was born in Birmingham, Alabama, in 1943. He first met Jimmy Johnson and Roger Hawkins while he was studying at the University of Alabama in Tuscaloosa in the early sixties. Beckett was self-taught on the piano and could not read music. That did not hider his aim of working as a musician. One of his first jobs in the music industry was working as a keyboardist in Pensacola, Florida, with the producer "Papa" Don Schroeder. He also played with the Esquires.

Schroeder brought Beckett to FAME Studios to play on a session with James and Bobby Purify in 1966. Hall was suitably impressed and soon offered Beckett a permanent job at his studio.

David Hood

The core of the new session band was almost complete. Rick Hall just needed a bass player and possibly a second guitarist.

David Hood was born in Sheffield, in the Shoals area, in 1943. He learned to play a variety of instruments at high school, including trombone, guitar and bass. During his studies at the University of North Alabama, he played with a group called the Mystics, whose members had all attended Sheffield High School. He later visited FAME Studios and played trombone on James & Bobby Purify's recording of "I'm Your Puppet" in 1966.

Rick Hall must have been impressed by that contribution and also by the versatility of a session man who could play at least three instruments. Hood was added to the session band.

Quin Ivy and Rick Hall soon called on his bass guitar skills for sessions with Percy Sledge and Etta James.

The future "Swampers" were now in place at FAME.

7

QUIN IVY: NORALA STUDIO

Quin Ivy was born in Oxford, Mississppi, in 1937. Like Rick Hall, he grew up in a share-cropping family. He took a job as a DJ on a local radio station, before moving to Memphis to join 1210 WMPS-AM. In 1959 he moved again, this time to Muscle Shoals, to DJ on WLAY-AM.

Rick Hall had just started working with Billy Sherrill and Tom Stafford at the little studio above the drugstore. One of his many promotional visits involved a stop at WLAY-AM, the station where Sam Phillips had worked and where now he met Quin Ivy.

Ivy soon moved on again, this time to WKDA-AM in Nashville, where he continued to receive visits from Hall. That experience served him well, as he was offered the job of top DJ back at WLAY-AM in 1961. The station had a policy of allowing the DJs to play a mix of music, with the intention of attracting black and white listeners. Black music was what Ivy liked to play most.

Given their similar backgrounds and their love of R&B music, it is not surprising that Ivy and Hall became friends. They started writing songs together, including two that were recorded at FAME by Jimmy Hughes: "I'm Qualified" and "Lollypops, Lace & Lipstick", the B-side of the hit single "Steal Away". Ivy also decided to open a record store in Sheffield on 2nd Street, which he called Tune Town.

Ivy watched Hall building his new FAME Studios and saw how the work slowly built up. He realized that, as more artists came to record there, so there was less need to fill the studio time with demo sessions, radio commercials and the like. By 1965 Hall was turning such work away, and Ivy saw an opportunity.

He asked Hall if he would mind if he (Ivy) opened a small studio, a bit like the old SPAR studio, near the record shop, to pick up some of the work that Hall could no longer fit in. Hall was happy with the idea.

Ivy duly opened his studio at a venue opposite his record store in 1965, calling it Norala Studio, short for Northern Alabama. He was able to buy an old RCA mono console from WLAY-AM for $150, adding an old Ampex 351 recorder and two old speakers.

He persuaded Hall to allow the FAME session musicians to come to Norala to play and tried to recruit Dan Penn too, as A&R man/engineer. Hall agreed that the musicians would be free to play at Norala, but he relied heavily on Penn and that request was turned down. Instead, Hall recommended Marlin Green for the role.

Marlin Greene was a talented musician who played trumpet and guitar. He had played with Dan Penn on occasions, in the Mark V and the Pallbearers, sitting in for Terry Thompson. Now he became Quin Ivy's right-hand-man, playing guitar, engineering, arranging and even designing the studio's logo.

It wasn't long before Ivy set up his own Norala label, on which the first single issued was a double A-sider by the Mosriters, featuring two instrumental tracks called "On the Run" and "Turmoil". The tracks were written by Don Srygley and Jimmy Johnson, who, along with David Hood and Roger Hawkins, were the four Mosriters. (Mosrite was the name of a Californian guitar company. The Ventures used Mosrite guitars on their hit instrumentals).

The second Norala single was another instrumental double-sider by the Mosriters, while the third was a vocal track by a young singer/songwriter from Muscle Shoals called Mickey Buckins. His song "Silly Girl" did not sell many copies, but he later joined FAME and went on to greater things.

Ivy was happy no doubt. He had his record store, his recording studio and his record label. He had access to some excellent session musicians and a very talented engineer. Now he just needed a talented singer.

In the summer of 1965, a band called the Esquires came to the studio. Their lead singer was Percy Sledge.

8

PERCY SLEDGE

Percy Tyrone Sledge was born in 1940 in Leighton, Alabama, not too far from the Shoals area. He worked for a while in Leighton, taking jobs in agriculture, before moving to Sheffield to become an orderly at Colbert County Hospital.

He had started singing at school and was recommended to the Esquires by one of his teachers. He worked during the week and at weekends he sang with the Esquires. A friend introduced him to Quin Ivy, who gave him an audition and signed the band.

Ivy particularly liked one of the band's songs, which Sledge had written with bassist Calvin Lewis and organist Andrew Wright. The song was called "Why Did You Leave Me". Quin Ivy and Marlin Greene decided to strengthen the lyrics and soon came up with a re-worked version of the original, which now had a new title: "When a Man Loves a Woman".

The Esquires had played on the session at first, but when the final recording was made, the band was made up of Spooner Oldham (organ), Roger Hawkins (drums), Junior Lowe (bass), Marlin Greene (lead guitar) and Don Srygley (rhythm guitar). The horn section was made up of three local musicians brought in by Ivy, Jack Peck, Billy Cofield and Don Pollard. Ivy and Greene were producing, and Jimmy Johnson was sound engineer.

Ivy was impressed with the final recording and played it to Rick Hall, who suggested that Jerry Wexler at Atlantic Records in New York should listen to it. Hall had promised Wexler that he would be alerted to any outstanding recordings in Muscle Shoals and now he kept that promise. He was confident that Wexler would be interested in marketing and distributing the song and he was not mistaken.

Wexler quickly offered Ivy $1000 and 8% of profits on the song. Ivy shared the percentage with Hall (1%) and Green (2%) and Sledge (3%). Hall received another 2% fee for "finding" the song from Wexler. For Ivy, the biggest gain was that Wexler agreed to promote and distribute more songs from Percy Sledge and other artists at Norala.

Percy Sledge in 1974

Photo: Gene Pugh (Wikimedia Commons)

There was just one small problem. Wexler wasn't happy with the horn section's contribution. He wanted a new version overdubbed, as he thought the original was out of tune. The master tape was sent to Memphis, where the Memphis Horns, Andrew Love and Wayne Jackson, augmented by Gene "Bowlegs" Miller, were called in and their version was added in place of the original. Given all that effort, it is a shame that the original tape was used by mistake instead of the Memphis Horns' version when the engineers cut the disc! The better version emerged much later, on a Rhino CD.

Nevertheless, with Wexler's backing and the national and international clout of Atlantic Records, Sledge's single took off. It was Atlantic's first gold single, topping the Billboard Hot

100 Singles Chart week-ending 28th May 1966 for two weeks and the Billboard Hot Rhythm & Blues Singles Chart for total of four weeks week-end 7th May 1966. It is interesting to note that Aretha Franklin had her first million-selling hit almost a year after Sledge, with "I Never Loved A Man (The Way I love You)". Sledge's song was also a hit in the UK, first in 1966, first when it reached number four on the Official UK Pop Singles Chart on 18th May 1966, remaining on the chart for seventeen weeks, and then again in 1987, when it went to number two on the UK Official Pop Single Chart on the 14th February 1987 and spent 10 weeks on the chart, following its inclusion in a Levi jeans ad. The single also achieved silver certification according to the BPI for over 200,000 copies sold in the UK, on the 1st March 1987. Sledge's voice was a perfect match for slow, emotional, Soul ballads, and Quin Ivy and Marlin Green now had the chance to build on that first big success for the little studio on 2nd Street. Wexler decided that the impact made by Sledge in the market, appealing to black and white listeners, justified investing in an album.

Percy Sledge at the Alabama Hall of Fame in 2010

Photo: Carol M. Highsmith (Wikimedia Commons)

Several songs had been recorded along with "When a Man Loves a Woman" and they were all included. The B-side was a Marlin Greene song "Love Me Like You Mean It", and to that were added "You're Pouring Water On a Drowning Man" and "You Fooled Me", a Dan Penn song. Seven more songs were recorded later in the year, with Peanutt Montgomery's "Love Me All The Way" one of the best. Altogether in 1966, Sledge released two albums and three singles, that established him as an international star. The two singles that followed that first hit song have also become iconic. "Warm and Tender Love" and "It Tears Me Up" both charted strongly. The single "Warm and Tender Love" became a Top 40 hit on the UK Official Pop Singles Chart going to number thirty-four on the 10th August 1966 and spending over seven weeks in the chart.

From 1965 to 1969, Sledge recorded regularly with Quin Ivy. Atlantic released sixteen of the tracks as singles, all of which entered the Hot 100.

Percy Sledge died in 2015 at his home in Baton Rouge, Louisiana. He has been honoured by many music organisations, including the Alabama Music Hall of Fame (1993), the Rock and Roll Hall of Fame (2005) and the Louisiana Music Hall of Fame 2007). In 1996 his album "Blue Night" was named the best Soul/Blues album of the year.

Recommended Tracks:

1966 Percy Sledge: "When a Man Loves a Woman"

1966 Percy Sledge: "Love Me All The Way"

1969 Percy Sledge: "Faithful and True"

1969 Percy Sledge: "True Love Travels On a Gravel Road"

9

WILSON PICKETT

Jerry Wexler had a problem to solve in 1966, when Stax Records co-owner Jim Stewart decided to withdraw his invitation to Wilson Pickett to record at Stax, where he had achieved some major successes working with Booker T & the MGs. Given the growing reputation of the studios in the Muscle Shoals area and the success of Percy Sledge, Wexler approached Rick Hall at FAME Studios, who welcomed Pickett to Alabama.

Pickett was not sure about the new set-up, with a white producer and a white session band. Segregation was strong in Alabama too. However, he trusted Wexler and began working with Spooner Oldham, Jimmy Johnson, Roger Hawkins and Tommy Cogbill.

By the end of 1966, Pickett had added two more hits to his growing collection. The first was "Land of 1000 Dances", released in May 1966, which went to number one on the Billboard R&B chart, number six on the US Pop chart and number twenty-two on the UK Pop chart. The second was "Mustang Sally", released in October, which reached number six on the R&B chart, number twenty-three on the US Pop chart and number twenty-eight on the UK Pop chart. Both singles won Pickett a gold disc from the RIAA. Pickett was convinced!

The following year saw the release of "Funky Broadway", also recorded by Pickett at FAME Studios. The Muscle Shoals magic was still intact. The single reached the top of the R&B chart, number eight on the Pop chart and entered the top fifty of the UK Pop chart. It was another gold disc for Pickett and for FAME Studios.

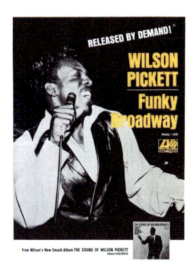

Wilson Pickett 1967

Atlantic Records Trade Ad (Wikimedia Commons)

He returned to FAME in late 1968 and worked with a session band featuring Duane Allman, Jerry Jemmott and Roger Hawkins. Pickett recorded several cover versions of well-known songs from the Pop charts, including "Hey Jude" and "Hey Joe", the first of which gave him a number sixteen hit on the UK Pop chart, with success in America too. The single reached number twenty-three on the US Pop chart and number thirteen R&B.

In 1971, Pickett came to FAME to record an album entitled "Don't Knock My Love". Three singles were released from the album that year, all of which sold well. The best of the three was "Don't Knock My Love, Pt. 1", which was awarded gold certification by the RIAA. It reached number thirteen on the Billboard Hot 100 Singles Chart and achieved the number one position on the Billboard Best Selling Soul Singles Chart week-ending 26th June 1971 (1 week), becoming Pickett's fifth R&B number one. The other two singles, "Call My Name, I'll Be There" and "Fire and Water" (originally a song recorded by the UK band Free), also entered the Pop and R&B charts.

The band on these sessions included David Hood, Roger Hawkins and Tippy Armstrong.

chart, becoming Pickett's fifth R&B number one. The other two singles, "Call My Name, I'll Be There" and "Fire and Water" (originally a song recorded by the UK band Free), also entered the Pop and R&B charts.

All in all, Jerry Wexler and Wilson Pickett must have been extremely happy with the switch to Muscle Shoals. The recordings made there were amongst the best of Pickett's career, certainly a match for the hits from Stax.

Rick Hall had equal reason to be happy, as the reputation of his studio grew, especially amongst the black R&B singers that he loved to record. There were some big names soon to follow in Pickett's footsteps.

Recommended Tracks:

1966 Wilson Pickett: "Land of 1000 Dances"

1966 Wilson Pickett: "Mustang Sally"

1967 Wilson Pickett: "Funky Broadway"

1971 Wilson Pickett: "Fire and Water"

10

ARTHUR CONLEY

Arthur Conley grew up in Atlanta, Georgia, where he joined a Gospel group, the Evening Smiles, at just twelve years of age. Soon after that, he formed an R&B group, Arthur & the Corvets, with whom he released a number of singles. In 1964, he made his first solo single, "I'm a Lonely Stranger", on the Ru-Jac label, which came to the attention of Otis Redding. Conley was still only eighteen, but Redding was impressed enough to invite him to Memphis, to re-record "I'm a Lonely Stranger" at Stax and to release the song on Redding's newly formed label Jotis Records. Another Jotis release "Who's Foolin' Who" followed in 1966.

At that point, Redding suggested a switch to FAME Records. Conley duly went to Muscle Shoals with Redding to sign for FAME, where a Dan Penn song "I Can't Stop (No, No, No)" was chosen as his first FAME release. The next release was Take Me (Just As I Am)", which Solomon Burke took into the charts the following year. The Conley version was equally good but had failed to make an impact. The music business can be very unfair at times!

Redding and Conley looked for inspiration and found it in the form of a Sam Cooke song "Yeah Man", which they started to adapt. They co-wrote a new version of the Cooke original, calling it "Sweet Soul Music", which was recorded at FAME in January 1967 and distributed on the Atco label.

The single rose to number two on both the Billboard Hot 100 Singles Chart and the Billboard Hot Rhythm & Blues Singles Chart. In the UK it went to number seven on the UK Singles chart, also charting in several other European markets. With total sales of over one million copies, "Sweet Soul Music" was awarded a gold disc by the RIAA.

Arthur Conley 1967

Photo: Atco Records Trade Ad (cropped) (Wikimedia Commons)

Sadly, the inspiration provided by Sam Cooke which had opened the gates to this major success also led to a problem. J.W. Alexander, Sam Cooke's business partner, sued Conley and Redding for stealing Cooke's melody. A settlement was reached, by which Cooke's name was added to the songwriting credits. In addition, Redding undertook to record some songs from Kags Music, a music publishing company that Cooke and Alexander had set up together. The outcome could have been much worse.

In 1967, two Arthur Conley albums were released on the Atco label, containing a mix of Jontis, FAME and Atco recordings. They are "Sweet Soul Music" and "Shake, Rattle & Roll". Otis Redding is credited as producer on both, with help from Jim Stewart and Rick Hall. Together the albums give an excellent overview of Conley's contribution to Soul music, combining a voice that sounds very like Sam Cooke and a style that is much influenced by Otis Redding. It would be hard to find two better models.

Conley came to live in the UK in 1970, before moving to Belgium and then the Netherlands, where he died in 2003.

Recommended Track:

1967 Arthur Conley: "Sweet Soul Music"

11
ARETHA FRANKLIN

Aretha Franklin was born in Memphis in 1942, but grew up in Detroit, where her father, C.L. Franklin, was a minister at the New Bethel Baptist Church. As a child she sang Gospel songs in the church and then began travelling to various churches to perform, with her father as manager. She signed to JVB Records and released her first single in 1956, a Gospel song entitled "Never Grow Old".

When she reached eighteen years of age, she told her father that she wanted to follow the example of Sam Cooke, recording secular music. Her father supported her decision and helped her make a demo disc to take to record companies. Sam Cooke suggested that she join RCA, like him, and Berry Gordy was also interesting in signing Aretha and her sister Erma to Motown, but her father preferred the offer from Columbia Records, who signed Aretha in 1960.

Despite releasing some good singles that charted on the national R&B chart, Aretha's success at Columbia was limited. The company didn't really know what style of music would suit her best.

When her contract expired in 1966, Jerry Wexler approached her and convinced her to join Atlantic Records. Wexler recognised that Aretha's Gospel background needed to be the foundation of her work at Atlantic. And he had seen how Wilson Pickett had responded to working at first at Stax Records in Memphis and then at FAME Studios in Muscle Shoals. He was confident that the FAME trick would also work with Aretha, allowing her to show the full expression of her talent.

Aretha Franklin arrived at FAME Studios in January 1967, carrying a Ronnie Shannon song that she wanted to record called "I Never Loved a Man (The Way I Love You)". When Aretha sat at the piano and started to sing, everyone knew they had struck gold. The studio band joined in, and the song was finished that same day. The single was released the following month and reached number one on the Billboard Hot Rhythm & Blues Singles Chart week-ending 25th March 1967 (7 weeks), while also peaking at number nine on the Billboard Hot 100 Singles Chart, giving Franklin the first top-ten Pop single of her solo career and first certified gold single.

Aretha Franklin 1967

Photo: Atlantic Records Trade Ad (cropped)

(Wikimedia Commons)

That, unfortunately for Rick Hall, was as good as it got. During the recording of Franklin's second song, a fight had broken out between Aretha's husband and manager Ted White and Ken Laxton, a member of the band. Rick Hall's intervention, trying to calm things down, seemed to make things worse.

Wexler aborted the sessions and took Aretha back to New York, where the album was completed, but with an interesting twist, typical of Wexler.

He invited some of the FAME studio band to come to New York to finish the recording. The plan duly worked and the album, which took its name from that first Muscle Shoals song, went gold. It was Aretha's tenth studio album, but she had finally found her real voice at Muscle Shoals, just as Wexler thought she would. Wexler was very good at his job! In 1967 he was named Record Executive of the Year for turning Aretha Franklin's career around.

The album contains a number of classic Aretha Franklin tracks, especially the title track and "Respect". The album was released in March 1967 and went to number two on the Billboard Album chart. The single "Respect" was number one on the Billboard Pop Singles chart for two weeks in June 1967, and number one on the R&B chart for eight weeks, from May to July 1967. It became Aretha's song! As Otis Redding acknowledged: "That little girl done took my song away from me". The song has also reverberated down the years as a feminist and civil rights anthem. Two more songs from the album's B side also stand out. "Do Right Woman, Do Right Man" was also recorded at FAME, although it was not completed when the altercation stopped the session. It was finished in New York on an eight-track machine and became the B-side of "I Never Loved a Man (The Way I Love You)". It was written by Dan Penn and Chips Moman, and Jerry Wexler was given the production credit.

When Jerry Wexler had arranged the visit to FAME, he had also arranged for Chips Moman and Tommy Cogbill to come from Memphis to join the session band. It was a strong group that came to the studio that day: Moman and Jimmy Johnson on guitars, Cogbill on bass, Roger Hawkins on drums, and Spooner Oldham on Wurlitzer electronic piano and Aretha on piano. The horn section consisted of Ken Laxton on trumpet, King Curtis and Charles Chalmers on tenor sax, and Willie Bridges on baritone sax.

For the sessions in New York, Ken Laxton was replaced by Melvin Lastie, and Gene Chrisman shared drum duties with Roger Hawkins. In addition, Aretha's sisters Carolyn and Erma along with Cissy Houston provided background vocals. Tom Dowd was responsible for arrangements and, along with Arif Mardin, did an excellent job as sound engineer.

The album was re-issued in 1969 in stereo.

Aretha Franklin went on to greater things, but she probably never forgot that day in January 1967, when she sat at the piano in the FAME Studio and played the first chord of "I Never Loved a Man (The Way I Love You)". The solo album "I Never Loved a Man (The Way I Love You)" became a certified gold album according to the RIAA on the 13th June 1967 and spent a total of 14 weeks at number one on the Billboard Soul and R&B Albums Chart week-ending 29th April 1967. According to Atlantic Records, the combined sales of the album and single was approximately 3.5 million copies that year in the USA. In the same year, the American music industry achieved the billion-dollar mark in gross earnings for the first time.

Franklin's first Grammy Award also came in 1967, for "Best Rhythm & Blues Recording and Best Rhythm & Blues Solo Vocal Performance, Female" for "Respect". The Recording Academy (the Grammy Award institution) stated that in the mid-1960s, Aretha Franklin was already a well-respected R&B soul singer. But her 1967 recording of the Otis Redding song "Respect", from her hit album "I Never Loved a Man (The Way I Love You)", went to number two on the Billboard 200 Album Chart listing, and to number one on the Billboard Soul and R&B Albums Chart, launching her to new heights of mainstream acclaim and popularity.

Recommended Tracks:

1967 Aretha Franklin: "I Never Loved a Man (The Way I Love You)"

1967 Aretha Franklin: "Do Right Woman, Do Right Man"

12

CLARENCE CARTER

Clarence Carter was born in 1936 in Montgomery, Alabama. He was blind from birth. In 1960 he graduated from Alabama State College in Montgomery with a degree in music. He taught himself guitar by listening to Blues guitarists, such as Jimmy Reed and John Lee Hooker, and could transcribe and arrange sheet music using Braille.

His first venture as a performer came as a member of a duo. He teamed up with a college friend, Calvin Scott, to form Clarence & Calvin, releasing several singles on the Fairlane label, before switching to Duke Records and simplifying the duo's name to the C & C Boys.

Following a few unsuccessful releases, the duo decided to try their luck at FAME Studios. They paid $85 to record "Step by Step" and the B-side "Rooster Knees and Rice" as a demo, which found its way to Jerry Wexler at Atlantic Records. Wexler was always on the look-out for new talent and decided to put the single out on the Atco label. Unfortunately, it met the fate of their earlier releases and Atlantic didn't sign them. The bad luck continued when Calvin Scott was badly injured in a car accident.

Clarence Carter decided to continue as a solo singer and was signed to FAME Records. Two singles were released in 1967, entitled "Tell Daddy" and "Thread the Needle", both of which entered the R&B chart, reaching number thirty-five and thirty-eight respectively. The second single crept into the Pop chart at number ninety-eight. "Tell Daddy" inspired a wonderful response from Etta James later in the year.

"Tell Daddy" was co-written with his touring band members William Armstrong, Marcus Daniel and Wilbur Terrell, with Carter receiving full writing credit. It was recorded at FAME

Studios in Muscle Shoals on 4th October 1966. On the recording session were legends of the Muscle Shoals Signature Sound David Hood (bass), Roger Hawkins (drums), Spooner Oldham (keyboards), and Memphis-born studio musician Marvell Thomas (keyboards). The single was released on the Cadet label, a division of Chess Records in August 1967.

The song starts with a powerful horns intro, accompanied by Hawkins' steady driving drumbeats. David Hood on bass responds to Hawkins' dynamic performing on drums, along with Spooner Oldham and Marvell Thomas on keyboards. Rick Hall using his brilliant sound engineering skills to create a classic up-tempo dancing style. The track also features the Memphis Horn Section and members of the future Muscle Shoals Horn section. "Tell Daddy" is an iconic masterpiece of Muscle Shoals Southern Soul, setting the template for future recordings at the studio.

At the end of 1967, Carter switched to Atlantic Records, while continuing to record at FAME.

The following year brought greater success with a single "Looking for a Fox" rising to number twenty on the R&B chart and number sixty-two on the Pop chart. Things were heading in the right direction, thanks once again to the work of Rick Hall and the FAME session band.

Carter's big breakthrough came in 1968, when his next single "Slip Away" reached number six on the Pop chart, number two on the R&B chart, and number one on the Cash Box Soul and R&B Singles Chart week-ending 31st August 1968 (1 week).

"Slip Away" has a dynamic bluesy guitar rhythm intro which continues with the same intense power right through recording, setting a pattern for future hit singles. The song's arrangement has steady bass and drumbeats, with a very emotional vocal performance by Carter, that is emphasized by the horn section, consisting of Gene "Bowlegs" Miller, Joe

Arnold and Aaron Varnell. These three were regularly used on recording sessions for Rick Hall at this time.

The song was released from Carter's studio album "This Is Clarence Carter" (1968) and was co-written by Clarence Carter's touring band members William Armstrong (keyboards), Marcus Daniel (bass), and Wilbur Terrell (drums).

Additional session musicians featured on the studio album are, from Memphis, Floyd Newman, James Mitchell (brother of Willie Mitchell of Hi Records fame) on baritone saxophone, along with Charles Chalmers and Andrew Love on tenor saxophone, and Wayne Jackson and Gene "Bowlegs" Miller on trumpet.

The following studio album, 1969's "Testifyin'", produced two Top Five R&B and Soul singles in the Southern Soul style. At the end of the year, he entered the Pop chart again with a Christmas song "Back Door Santa", which made it to number four. Co-written by Carter himself and Marcus Daniel, this song in my view is the funkiest that Carter ever recorded. The band is led by an aggressive rhythm guitar performance by Albert "Junior" Lowe, with Roger Hawkins on drums and a driving bass line by David Hood or Jesse Boyce holding the rhythm section together in a raw and refined style. The dynamic horn section gives the song a very Memphis feel, with Ronnie Eades on baritone sax, Aaron Varnell and Joe Arnold on tenor sax, and Gene "Bowlegs" Miller and Harrison Calloway on trumpet.

Two more studio albums followed, "The Dynamic Clarence Carter" (1969) and "Patches" (1970). The first of these was the first album by Carter to feature string arrangements and background vocals. The string arrangements were written by William Fischer, an African American, and the background vocals on track four were performed by Alvin Willford, Cabwhiss Grandberry and James Price. The Swampers were joined by Duane Allman on lead guitar and Marvell Thomas on organ. The single "Too Weak To Fight" was released from the album, reaching number thirteen Pop and number three R&B. Like "Slip Away", it was certified gold by the RIAA.

The "Patches" album is more sophisticated, with a dynamic string arrangement by Jimmy Haskell, a well-known composer of film soundtrack scores. Rick Hall hired Haskell to create a lush sound that was becoming popular amongst African American artists who wanted to cross over into the Pop album charts. The backing vocals also added to the sophistication. They were provided by Charles Chalmers, Donna Rhodes and Sandy Rhodes, who would later feature on classic Al Green recordings at Hi Records in Memphis, working with Willie Mitchell.

With the second FAME session band now departed, the session musicians on the album were members of the FAME Gang. Cornell McFadden, Freeman Brown and Fred Pouty shared drumming duties, with Junior Lowe, Clarence Carter and Travis Wammack on guitar, and Jesse Boyce, Bob Wray and Jerry Masters on bass. Clayton Ivey played keyboards. The horn section consisted of Ronnie Eades (baritone sax), Aaron Varnell and Harvey Thompson (tenor sax), and Jack Peck and Harrison Calloway Jr. (trumpet). The latter was also responsible for the horn arrangements.

The album contains a number of memorable tracks, including a cover of the Beatles' classic "Let It Be" with wonderful backing vocals from Rhodes, Chalmers, Rhodes. "Willie & Laura-Mae Jones" (written by Tony Joe White) is a good example of Country Soul, an up-tempo ballad based on memories of living in a small community. There is a real warmth in the singing and playing, with soft guitar, rich horns and strong backing vocals, all driven along by a bouncy piano line. "Patches", released as a single, was also a moving

Country Soul ballad, a style that suited Carter very much indeed.

Clarence Carter

Photo: John Mathew Smith & www.celebrity-photos.com

(Wikimedia Commons)

Importantly, Carter was able to build some strong momentum through 1969 and 1970. Seven more singles were released during this period, six of which entered the top thirteen of the R&B Chart. All seven made the top 100 on the Pop chart. The most successful of these songs was "Patches", which took Carter to new heights. The song reached number one on the Cash Box R&B Soul Singles Chart, week-ending 5th September 1970. It peaked at number four on the Billboard Hot 100 Pop chart and number two on the Billboard R&B chart. It was also a big hit in Australia and the UK, where it reached number two on the Singles chart, making it FAME Records most successful UK release. Within two months of its issue, the song had sold a million copies, bringing Carter and

Rick Hall another gold disc. Best of all, the song won the 1971 Grammy for best R&B song.

The song was written by the Detroit songwriting legends General Johnson and Ron Dunbar. It tells the story of life in the deep South for poor families, black and white, where the breadwinner dies, an echo of Rick Hall's own story.

Rick Hall, Clarence Carter and Jerry Wexler at Atlantic must have thought that this would herald further successful releases but, this time around, it proved harder to maintain that level of success and Carter left Atlantic Records at the end of 1971 to rejoin FAME Records. Only four singles were released over the next four years, with just two making it into the top twenty on the R&B chart. In 1975, Carter moved on again, to ABC Records, but failed to re-ignite his career in terms of chart success. He continued to tour and has remained popular, especially in the southern States.

Recommended Tracks:

1968 Clarence Carter: "Looking For a Fox"

1968 Clarence Carter: "Slip Away"

1968 Clarence Carter: "Too Weak To Fight"

1970 Clarence Carter: "Patches"

13

JAMES AND BOBBY PURIFY

James and Bobby Purify came to FAME Studios from Florida in 1966 to record an album. They had been signed by Don Schroeder to Bell Records and were looking to break into the Pop market. The two singers, James Lee Purify and Robert Lee Dickey, were cousins, but Dickey took the stage name of Purify to simplify things.

They began by teaming up with Dan Penn, who suggested a song for their first single that he had written with Spooner Oldham, called "I'm Your Puppet". It was released in September 1966, with "So Many Reasons" (written by Penn with Marlin Greene) on the B-side, and went on to sell one million copies, spending fourteen weeks on the charts and reaching number five R&B and number six on the Pop chart.

The album, "James & Bobby Purify", was issued in 1967, along with a second single, "Wish You Didn't Have to Go", another Penn/ Oldham composition which also charted, reaching number thirty-eight on the Pop chart and number twenty-seven on the R&B chart.

The album has an interesting selection of songs, mixing some Sam Cooke and Otis Redding tracks with a Wilson Pickett number. The session band was a strong one, featuring David Hood (bass), Roger Hawkins (drums), Jimmy Johnson and Junior Lowe (guitars), Spooner Oldham (piano and vibraphone), Ed Logan (saxophone and flute), and Charles Chalmers (saxophone). Don Schroeder took charge of production, with Rick Hall as sound engineer.

The success of the visit to FAME led to a second album being released in 1967, entitled "The Pure Sound of the Purifys". Two of the tracks were recorded at FAME, with the remaining songs the work of Chips Moman and his team at American Sound Studios in Memphis. The FAME songs are "Goodness Gracious", written by Schroeder and Oldham, and "Hello There" from the pen of Dan Penn.

Recommended Track:

1967 James & Bobby Purify: "So Many Reasons"

14

ARTISTS FROM CHESS RECORDS AT FAME

A series of artists signed to Chess Records in Chicago also came to FAME Studios between 1967 and 1969 to find success. They were following in the footsteps of Aretha Franklin and Wilson Pickett, who had both come to FAME with a similar intention and left with major hit songs.

Jerry Wexler at Atlantic Records had seen the potential of Rick Hall's studio, when Jim Stewart at Stax Records decided to terminate the arrangement that had brought Atlantic artists to Memphis. Wexler switched Wilson Pickett to FAME in 1966, where he recorded two major hits before the year ended. Aretha followed at the start of 1967 and had come alive there. She would undoubtedly have recorded many more tracks there, had it not been for the altercation that occurred.

Rick Hall had established good links with Chess Records in Chicago during the mid-sixties, when several songs recorded at FAME were licensed to Chess for distribution. Now, Hall offered them the opportunity to send their own artists to FAME, to possibly enjoy the success that Pickett and Franklin had found there. The reputation of the second FAME session band was big enough now to persuade Leonard Chess to send Irma Thomas to work with Rick Hall and his team.

Then came Maurice and Mac, followed by Etta James and Laura Lee. Other less well-known artists also came to record, including Bobby Moore & the Rhythm Aces, Mitty Collier and Lee Webber.

Irma Thomas

Irma Thomas visited Muscle Shoals in 1967. Despite being signed to a Chicago label, she was the Soul Queen of New

Orleans. She had begun her recording career with Ron Records, achieving a number twenty-two R&B hit with "Don't Mess With My Man" in 1959. Soon after that, she signed to Minit Records in New Orleans and worked with Allen Toussaint, releasing several R&B hit singles. When Minit was bought by Imperial, the hits continued, the biggest of which was "Wish Someone Would Care" in 1964. Despite these successes, Irma Thomas was not able to break through into the Pop market. She remained popular in the South, around New Orleans, but was seeking greater exposure. She signed with Chess Records in Chicago in 1967 and came to Muscle Shoals in search of some Rick Hall magic.

Irma Thomas 2008

Photo: Definitiv (Wikimedia Commons)

During June and July of 1967, Thomas recorded thirteen tracks at FAME Studios, in preparation for an album release on the Chess label. The track "Cheater Man" was released in 1967 to test the market, but there was no big breakthrough. Two further tracks appeared as single releases in 1968, "A Woman Will Do Wrong" and a cover of the Otis Redding song

"Good To Me". The last of the three did enter the R&B chart, but Chess were not happy with the results and Thomas moved on to California. The plans for an album release were dropped.

The ten remaining tracks stayed in the vaults at Chess Records until 1984, when an album of the Muscle Shoals songs, featuring twelve tracks, was released in Japan (Chess, P-Vine Special).

In 1990, Chess/MCA Records released another compilation of the Muscle Shoals songs, featuring fourteen tracks. The extra track is an alternate mix of "We Got Something Good". The compilation is called "Something Good/The Muscle Shoals Sessions".

Just to complicate things, an extended version of the Japanese album was released in Europe in 1991, with all thirteen songs included (Chess, Charly Records). The album is presented as a compilation, entitled "Down At Muscle Shoals".

The FAME session band who played with Irma Thomas were David Hood and Tommy Cogbill, who shared bass duties, Roger Hawkins on drums, Jimmy Johnson on guitar, and Spooner Oldham on keyboards. The horn section included some later members of the Muscle Shoals horns. Rick Hall was in charge of production.

The track listing begins with the three single releases. "Cheater Man" is a Dann Penn/Spooner Oldham composition with a strong Memphis feel. Track two "A Woman Will Do Wrong", written by Paul Kelly and Clarence Reid, is a slow ballad, featuring a harmony vocal and a strong sax line. For the third song, "Good To Me", Thomas sings with more expression, but Otis is a hard act to follow! Thomas' version starts with a low-key horn intro, with a soft, tender vocal. The romantic feeling is heightened by the angelic backing voices, the smooth horn section and the gentle tempo set by the drums. The song slowly gathers pace and builds to its crescendo.

The previously unreleased tracks start with "We Got Something Good". This is one of the strongest songs on the album, written by Maurice Dollison, with an up-tempo, bouncy tune and punchy horns. Track five is another Penn/Oldham song, "Let's Do It Over", a good example of Muscle Shoals Soul, which suits Thomas' voice more than some of the others on the album. "I Gave You Everything", written by Larry Hamby and Terry Woodford, demonstrates this well. Thomas tries to add a rough edge to her voice, but the result is not convincing.

Track seven, "I've Been Loving You Too Long", is another Otis Redding song, co-written with Jerry Butler. Thomas follows the original closely, and the session band provide a solid backing, but, as before, Otis' version is just unbeatable. "Security", the next track, repeats the pattern, with more success. Thomas is more at ease with the tempo. Track nine is "Somewhere Crying", written by Oliver Sain Jr. It was the B-side of the "Cheater Man" single. It is a deep soul ballad, one of the best songs on the album, which shows Thomas' voice at its best and illustrates the strengths of the rhythm and horn sections. It also features Spooner Oldham on organ, adding his signature sound which is a key aspect of the Muscle Shoals sound. The next track "Don't Make Me Stop Now" is another song which suits Thomas' voice. She softens her delivery and stresses the romantic nature of the lyric. For track eleven Thomas chose another Penn/Oldham song entitled "Good Things Don't Come Easy", followed by "Here I Am, Take Me". Both are typical Muscle Shoals Soul songs. The thirteenth song recorded at the 1967 sessions is "Yours Until Tomorrow", written by Goffin and King, another slow ballad.

Thirty-two years after the FAME sessions, Irma Thomas made another Southern Soul album. It was recorded in Memphis at Sounds Unreel in September 1999. The subsequent album,

"My Heart's In Memphis", is a collection of Dan Penn songs, all written with various collaborators, including Spooner Oldham, Donny Fritts and Irma Thomas herself. It was released in 2000 by Rounder Records. It is a Memphis album, but the memory of Muscle Shoals is evident. Certainly, the relaxed style of the songs and Thomas' softer delivery are a long way from Memphis and much nearer the Shoals' sound. In 1967 Irma Thomas was still young and learning the trade. In 1999 she sings with confidence, in a lower register. The rather shrill vocal lines of some of the earlier songs, where Thomas seemed to be forcing things, are now smooth and easy.

Recommended Tracks:

1968 Irma Thomas: "A Woman Will Do Wrong"

1968 Irma Thomas: "Good To Me" (both recorded 1967)

Maurice and Mac

Maurice McAlister and McLauren Green were both members of the Radiants, a group formed in 1960 by members of the choir at the Greater Harvest Baptist Church in Chicago. They left the group in 1966 and recorded their first single as a duo on the Chess subsidiary label, Checker Records. It failed to create any real interest.

Maurice and Mac were then sent down to FAME Studios to record their second single, a cover of a Dan Penn, Oscar Franck, Rick Hall song, "You Left the Water Running", which was released by Chess, again on the Checker label, in 1968. The original version was recorded at FAME by Wilson Pickett, based on a demo that Otis Redding had done at Rick Hall's request. The Maurice and Mac version is slick and funky, inviting you to tap your feet and join in with the song. It has a feel-good bouncy rhythm and some good harmonies. It is not in the Soul style of Otis Redding's version, but it is a classic of Muscle Shoals R&B. The horns, the organ and the Blues guitar combine beautifully; everybody is having a lot of fun on that session. The single was on the Cashbox chart for three weeks, and that was as good as it got for the two Chicago boys. Two more single releases recorded in Chicago failed to sell, and they moved on.

They had in fact recorded seven songs at FAME, only one of which had seen the light of day. Then, in 1984, just as with Irma Thomas, a compilation album of their songs appeared in Japan, entitled "Lean On Me" (Chess/P-Vine Special). The album contains all seven of the Muscle Shoals tracks on the second side, combined with seven Chicago tracks on side one.

The FAME songs are all worth a listen. There are two Soul ballads, "You're the One" and "So Much Love" (written by Goffin and King), beautifully sung with good harmonies. The steady drumbeat and soft horns are typical of FAME.

"Love Power" and "Try Me" are up-tempo songs, presented in the style of Sam & Dave. "Why Don't You Try Me" (not to be confused with "Try Me") is a Billy Young song that features a typical FAME organ in the mix. The church-like feel suggests that Spooner Oldham joined the session. "Lean On Me" is obviously not the Bill Withers song from 1972, but a power ballad, with an interesting backing led by piano and organ.

"You Left the Water Running" is the stand-out track, but all seven songs are strong. It is incomprehensible that Chess chose to release only one track.

Recommended Tracks:

1968 Maurice and Mac: "You Left the Water Running"

1968 Maurice and Mac: "Lean On Me"

Etta James

Etta James was the next Chess Records artist who came to FAME to record an album during 1967, in search of a boost for her career which had gone into decline. Between 1960 and 1965, she had recorded five studio albums at Chess Records in Chicago, all released on the Argo label. In 1966 the six, "Call My Name", appeared on Cadet, produced by Leonard Chess. None of them had charted except the first, "At Last".

Rick Hall had good contacts with the Chicago music companies and must have been confident that Etta James would enjoy working at FAME. Leonard Chess agreed and encouraged James to embrace the opportunity.

In Chicago James had worked with the Chess brothers, covering a range of genres, ranging from Jazz through classic ballads to Blues, Rock and Soul. Chess had tried to market her as the Chicago Queen of Soul, but she was much more than that.

At FAME, the songs she chose reflect her amazing ability to do justice to all kinds of material, and in the FAME session band, she found a group of musicians who had a similar range of abilities. On keyboards were Spooner Oldham and George Davis, with Barry Beckett and Carl Banks on organ, Marvell Thomas on piano, David Hood on bass guitar, Roger Hawkins on drums, and Junior Lowe and Jimmy Ray Jenkins on guitar. The horn section featured Gene "Bowlegs" Miller on trumpet, James Mitchell and Aaron Varnell on saxophone, and Floyd Newman on baritone sax. Charles Chalmers sang background vocals. Rick Hall took care of production.

By the end of the sessions, James had recorded twenty-two songs. Twelve tracks were chosen for inclusion on the album that resulted from the visit.

Etta James in Deauville 1990

Photo: Roland Godefroy (Wikimedia Commons)

Track One is the title song, "Tell Mama", written by Clarence Carter, Marcus Daniel and Wilbur Terrell. Track Two is a song originally credited to Billy Foster, a friend of James, but she later explained the song's origin in different terms in her autobiography *Rage To Survive.* The song was co-written by James herself, following a prison visit to see another friend Ellington Jordan. He outlined the song to her, and she helped him to finish it. That finished song has become a Blues standard: "I'd Rather Go Blind".

Also included on the album are songs by Jimmy Hughes, Charles Chalmers, Rick Hall and Spooner Oldham, giving the album a strong Muscle Shoals foundation. There is also a flavour of Memphis, with songs from Otis Redding and Rosco Gordon, and two songs from Don Covay, who had written songs at Stax with Steve Cropper, Booker T. Jones and David Porter.

The album took Etta James back into the charts in 1968, reaching number twenty-one on the Billboard R&B Albums chart and number eighty-two on the Pop chart.

Two singles were released from the album, both of which sold well. "Tell Mama" went to number ten on the R&B Singles chart and number twenty-three on the Pop chart. "Security", a cover of the Otis Redding song, went to number eleven (R&B) and number thirty-five (Pop). In addition, "I'd Rather Go Blind" has become an absolute classic, with the recent version by Joe Bonamassa and Beth Hart outstanding.

The album was re-issued in the 1990s, having been remastered in California at Universal Mastering Studios-West by Erick Labson.

A further release came in 2001, this time a compilation of all twenty-two of the songs recorded at Muscle Shoals. Amongst the added tracks are covers of David Houston's "Almost Persuaded", Sonny & Cher's "I Got You Babe" and Aretha Franklin's "Do Right Woman, Do Right Man", which Chips Moman and Dan Penn had written. This version of the album is called "Tell Mama: The Complete Muscle Shoals Sessions".

It seems likely that Etta James and Leonard Chess were aware of the impact that FAME Studios had had on Aretha Franklin and on Wilson Pickett too. It was hard to argue with the successful output of those artists and, given James' wide-ranging talent, it was no surprise when "Tell Mama" turned out so well for her too.

Sadly, Etta James didn't record at Muscle Shoals again. She did however make a wonderful album of soulful ballads entitled "Life's Been Rough On Me", released in 1997, with Barry Beckett on keyboards and in charge of production. It is well worth a listen.

Recommended Tracks:

1968 Etta James: "Tell Mama"

1968 Etta James: "I'd Rather Go Blind"

1968 Etta James: "Do Right Woman, Do Right Man"

(all recorded in 1967)

Laura Lee

Laura Lee was born in Chicago in 1945 but grew up in Detroit. Her mother, Ernestine Rundless, was a Gospel singer, who founded the Meditation Singers group. In 1956, Laura joined the group, replacing the original lead singer Della Reese, remaining until 1965, when she decided to move to a career in secular music as a solo artist. She cut her first single for Ric-Tic Records in 1966, a song entitled "To Win Your Heart", before moving to Chess Records in 1967. After recording a few songs with her in Chicago, the Chess team decided to send her to FAME to record.

Chess released seven Laura Lee singles during the two years she was signed to them, with five of them being recorded at FAME, produced by Rick Hall and backed by FAME's second group of session musicians. "Dirty Man"/ "It's Mighty Hard" and "Wanted: Lover, No Experience Necessary"/ "Up Tight, Good Man" appeared in 1967, followed the next year by "Hang It Up"/ "It's How You Make It Good", "Need To Belong"/ "He Will Break Your Heart", and "As Long As I Got You"/ "A Man With Some Backbone".

Lee switched briefly to Atlantic Records in 1969 and then moved swiftly on to Hot Wax, a subsidiary of Holland, Dozier, Holland's Invictus label in Detroit. Later in her career, she returned to Gospel music and was ordained as a minister.

Most of the songs that she recorded during the FAME sessions were written by Chess songwriters, including Bobby Miller, Leonard Caston and Lloyd Webber. "As Long As I Got You" is a Gene Barge song, co-written with Laura herself, and "It's Mighty Hard" is a James Cleveland song. "Need To Belong" is a Curtis Mayfield song. Just three of the songs on the five FAME singles released by Chess were written or co-written by songwriters at FAME. "Up Tight Good Man" is a Dan Penn/Spooner Oldham composition, "A Man With Some Backbone" was written by Clarence Carter and Marcus Daniel, and "He Will Break Your Heart" was co-written by Clarence Carter, Jerry Butler and Curtis Mayfield. All these songs fitted Laura Lee's style very well. The subject matter too was spot on; Laura Lee's songs often had a lot to say about how women were treated in life.

There were other songs recorded at the sessions that Chess chose to leave in the can. Three are of particular interest to fans of Muscle Shoals Soul and R&B, "Sure As Sin", "It's All Wrong But It's All Right", and "It Ain't What You Do". The first two were written by Marlin Greene and Eddie Hinton, who worked at Norala Studio with Quin Ivy. Hinton had brought the songs to FAME in the hope that Rick Hall would suggest them to visiting artists, and that indeed is what happened. During her two-week session in early 1968, Hall recommended the songs to Laura Lee, who cut excellent versions of them with the FAME session band.

Two good versions of "Sure As Sin" were released, one by Jeannie Greene, Marlin's wife, and the other by Candi Staton, but Lee's version didn't appear until 1984 on the compilation album "Up Tight Good Woman" (Chess/ P-Vine Special), released in Japan. The song subsequently featured on two further albums, "That's How It Is" in 1990 and "Chess Sing A Song Of Soul #5" in 2018. It was worth the wait! Laura Lee's version is powerful and dramatic, with excellent arrangements for the horns and a typical Spooner Oldham organ part. The Japanese compilation album notes make it clear that Lee recorded fourteen songs at FAME Studios, which are all included on the album.

"It's All Wrong But It's All Right" is a Soul ballad, that appeared on Percy Sledge's 1968 album "Take Time To Know Her". Lee's version loses nothing in comparison. Once again, Chess held on to the recording for a number of years before eventually including it on the 1972 Laura Lee compilation album "Love More Than Pride", and then including it again on several more compilation albums.

"It Ain't What You Do" was written by Jimmy Hughes, who had recorded "Steal Away" the first hit single made at the Avalon Road FAME Studio in 1964. Hughes' original version of the song appeared in 1967 on the Atlantic label. Lee's version has a different arrangement, which works well. Her punchy delivery is nicely augmented by the band, who create a very Stax-like sound. It is included on the Chess Laura Lee retrospective album "That's How It Is" released in 1990.

Recommended Tracks:

1967 Laura Lee: "Wanted, Lover, No Experience Necessary"

1972 Laura Lee: "It's All Wrong But It's Alright" (recorded 1968)

Other Chess Artists

Some lesser-known Chess artists also made the trip to FAME in 1967 or 1968. They were Bobby Moore & the Rhythm Aces, Mitty Collier and Lee Webber.

Bobby Moore was a tenor sax player, who led his own band. He was a native of New Orleans but was stationed at Fort Benning in Georgia whilst on military service, where he formed the Rhythm Aces. In 1961 he left the army and moved to Montgomery, Alabama. The Rhythm Aces got a new line-up and played with Sam Cooke and Ray Charles when they came on tour. The band recorded a song called "Searching For My Love" in 1965 at the FAME Studios, which Rick Hall took to the Chess brothers in Chicago, who decided to buy the rights to the recording. It was duly released on the Checker label and entered the charts, reaching number seven on the R&B chart and number twenty-seven on the Billboard Hot 100 in 1966, selling over a million copies. Two further singles just made it into the charts, but when their fourth single didn't sell well, the group was dropped by Chess. They continued to perform in and around Alabama.

Mitty Collier was born in Birmingham, Alabama, in 1941. She started singing in church and joined two Gospel groups, before deciding to raise money towards her education by singing R&B songs in local clubs. During a visit to Chicago in 1959, she entered a talent show, which she won for six consecutive weeks. The prize was an appearance on the same bill as B.B. King and Etta James, which led to a contract with Chess Records. Her first recordings for Chess took place in 1961 and she stayed with them until 1968.

The last song that Collier recorded for Chess was a new version of "Gotta Get Away From It All", which she had originally recorded in Chicago in 1961. The new version was produced by Rick Hall at FAME Studios. Unfortunately, the single didn't make any impression and Collier moved to Peachtree Records in Atlanta.

Recommended Track:

1968 Mitty Collier: "Got To Get Away From It All"

Lee Webber also recorded one single at FAME in 1968. The A-side is a Penn/Oldham composition called "Party Time" and the B-side is Alabama R&B version of the Lennon/McCartney song "Good Day Sunshine". The Penn/Oldham song is an up-tempo dance track, and the Beatles cover is a very unusual version, reconfigured as a Soul song. Webber left Chess soon after and only has one more single to his name. "Your Love's So Good" was recorded in 1973 for Excello Records, with "Seventh Son" on the B-side.

The last musician to consider in this chapter is **Charles Chalmers**. He came to FAME in 1967, while signed to Chess

Records, to make a largely instrumental album with Rick Hall, "Sax & the Single Girl". The tracks are a mixture of Pop hits and Soul tunes, starting with a Penn/Oldham song "Take Me (Just As I Am)". The Muscle Shoals connection is reinforced by the inclusion of Terry Thompson's "Night Rumble" and "Two In The Morning", written by Junior Lowe, Spooner Oldham and Roger Hawkins.

The session band for the album was a strong group, with David Hood on bass, Roger Hawkins on drums, Junior Lowe and Jimmy Johnson on guitar, Carly Banks on organ, Spooner Oldham on piano, and an excellent horn section made up of Floyd Newman on baritone sax, Aaron Varnell, Charles Chalmers and Andrew Love on tenor sax, and Gene Miller and Wayne Jackson on trumpet. Rick Hall was producer and engineer.

Chalmers was a Memphis musician and was already well-known at FAME when he came to record his album. He had been engaged by Rick Hall to play saxophone on the Wilson Pickett sessions that produced "Land of 1000 Dances" and "Mustang Sally". During those sessions, Chalmers had met Jerry Wexler and Tom Dowd from Atlantic Records, who later called on Chalmers to play with Aretha Franklin. He went on to record with Etta James, Clarence Carter, Millie Jackson, Dorothy Moore (at Malaco Records) and a host of other artists from a wide range of genres.

Chalmers is best known for his work at Hi Records in Memphis, first as a sax player but then as a backing vocalist, alongside Sandra and Donna Rhodes. Willie Mitchell was responsible for that. He asked Chalmers to organize a session with Sandra and Donna as backing singers, but Mitchell didn't feel that their vocals were strong enough. He suggested that Chalmers join them, and the results made Mitchell happy. The song was "Let's Stay Together", Al Green's mega-hit.

Chalmers went on to work with Frank Sinatra in Las Vegas, before moving to Miami, where he worked with the Bee Gees and K.C. & the Sunshine Band. In 1989 he moved to Branson, Missouri, where he built his own studio.

"Reaching Out: Chess Records at Fame Studios" on the Kent label

(used with permission of Ace Records UK)

In 2015, Ace Records issued a compilation album on their Kent label, featuring twenty-four of the songs that Chess artists had recorded at FAME Studios. Three of the songs were previously unreleased. It is presented as a tribute to Chess artists, but it is also a fascinating collection that demonstrates the genius of Rick Hall and the session players at FAME. The tracks all date from 1967 to 1969; fans around the world have waited a long time for a small UK company to make them available!

This is the track listing for "Reaching Out: Chess Records at Fame Studios".

1. It's All Wrong But It's Alright - Laura Lee
2. So Much Love - Maurice & Mac
3. Good To Me - Irma Thomas
4. The Same Rope - Etta James
5. Wanted, Lover; No Experience Necessary - Laura Lee
6. Reaching Out - Bobby Moore And The Rhythm Aces
7. The Sidewinder - Charles Chalmers
8. Security - Etta James
9. Run To Me - Maurice & Mac
10. Too Soon To Know - Mitty Collier
11. Good Day Sunshine - Lee Webber
12. Don't Lose Your Good Thing - Etta James
13. Two In The Morning - Charles Chalmers
14. Hang It Up - Laura Lee
15. Lean On Me - Maurice & Mac
16. Let's Do It Over - Irma Thomas
17. I Wanna Be Your Man - Bobby Moore & The Rhythm Aces
18. Sure As Sin - Laura Lee
19. Party Time - Lee Webber
20. Take Me (Just As I Am) - Charles Chalmers
21. You're Living A Lie - Mitty Collier
22. It's How You Make It Good - Laura Lee
23. A Woman Will Do Wrong - Irma Thomas
24. Come Back Baby - Bobby Moore And The Rhythm Aces

Hats off to the folks at Ace Records who tracked down these great songs!

15

CANDI STATON

Canzetta Maria Staton, known as Candi, was born in 1940 in Hanceville, Alabama. She started singing in a Gospel group at the age of eight. In the early fifties Candi and her sister Maggie went to Nashville to attend the Jewell Christian Academy, where they formed the Jewell Gospel Trio alongside Naomi Harrison. The trio were able to perform on the Gospel circuit, appearing with Mahalia Jackson, Aretha Franklin, C.L. Franklin (Aretha's father), the Staple Singers and the Soul Stirrers. They made several recordings between 1953 and 1963, which were released on Nashboro, Apollo or Savoy Records.

Towards the end of the sixties, Staton decided to follow the route taken by Sam Cooke and Aretha Franklin (and many others) away from Gospel music, in search of a career based on secular music. She started singing in a club in Birmingham and it was there that she was spotted by Clarence Carter. He introduced her to Rick Hall, who invited her to FAME Studios to sing, first as a background vocalist and then as a solo performer.

Staton's first FAME Records release was a single called "'I'd Rather Be An Old Man's Sweetheart (Than A Young Man's Fool)', written by Clarence Carter, George Jackson and Raymond Moore. It reached number forty-six on the Pop chart and number nine on the R&B chart in 1969. Two more singles were issued that year; "I'm Just a Prisoner (Of Your Good Lovin')" and "Never in Public", with the first of these charting at number fifty-six Pop and number sixteen R&B.

Over the next three years there were five more successful singles, all of which entered the Pop and R&B charts. These were "Sweet Feeling" and "Stand By Your Man" in 1970, and "He Called Me Baby" (1971), "In the Ghetto" (1972) and "Do It in the Name of Love" (1973). The first three all made the top ten of the R&B Chart. All these tracks were produced by Rick Hall and recorded with the FAME session band. During the same period, Staton released three albums on the FAME label, entitled "I'm Just a Prisoner", "Stand By Your Man" and "Candi Staton".

Staton had made a solid start to her career, with a lot of support from Clarence Carter, whom she married in 1970. Her cover versions of "Stand By Your Man" and "In the Ghetto" were both nominated for Grammy awards. She appeared on *Soul Train* in 1972 and she had also acquired a nickname as the First Lady of Southern Soul. Everything seemed set for a bright future. 1973 saw the release of two more singles. The first was "Love Chain", a George Jackson song, which reached number thirty-one on the R&B chart. The second was "Something's Burning", written by Mac Davis, which reached number eighty-three R&B.

Candi Staton at Guilfest 2012

Photo: Alex Marshall (Wikimedia Commons)

In 1974, Staton switched from FAME Records to Warner Bros. At first, she continued to work with Rick Hall, but from 1975 she started working with producer David Crawford. It was from this collaboration that a big hit emerged in 1976. The song "Young Hearts Run Free", written by Crawford, reached number one on the Hot Soul 100 chart and number twenty on the Billboard Hot 100 chart. In the UK, it went to number two on the Singles chart.

In 1982, Staton returned to Gospel, releasing a series of inspirational albums, broken in 1986 by a single "You Got the Love" made with the Source, which sold over two million copies. In 2004 a UK record label Honest Jon's issued a compilation album of Staton's best Soul songs from the early part of her career, which sold very well. A follow-up album came from the same company in 2006, entitled "These Hands", with a third appearing in 2009, "Who's Hurting Now?". The success of these albums gave Staton the chance to team up once more with Rick Hall, to record a number of tracks for her 2014 album "Life Happens", thus bringing the story back to FAME.

Candi Staton's "Evidence" compilation on the Kent label

(used with permission of Ace Records UK)

"Evidence", the Ace Records compilation released on the Kent label in 1111, contains forty-eight tracks recorded at FAME with Rick Hall. In an interview for Soul Express, Staton has spoken of the impact that Hall had on her career: "Rick knows exactly what he wants, and he doesn't stop until he gets it. I was in my twenties, but he made me sing songs over and over and over again. He wanted to get that hoarseness in my voice. When we recorded, everybody was in the same room together and everybody would be looking at each other. Maybe I would do something with my voice and Jimmy Johnson, the guitar player, would just feel me. Nowadays, when you do everything on keyboards, you don't really get that feeling and the connection like you used to. That's what made that music so fantastic."

Recommended Tracks:

1969 Candi Staton: "Never In Public"

1970 Candi Staton: "That's How Strong My Love Is"

1970 Candi Staton: "How Can I Put Out The Flame (When You Keep The Fire Burning)"

1971 Candi Staton: "What Would Become of Me"

1972 Candi Staton: "In The Ghetto"

1972 Candi Staton: "The Thanks I Get For Loving You"

16

HISTORY REPEATS ITSELF

A key event occurred at FAME in 1969 when the core members of Rick Hall's studio band (David Hood on bass, Jimmy Johnson on guitar, Roger Hawkins on drums and Barry Beckett on keyboards) departed from the FAME Studios organisation to set up their own studios and production facilities down the road at 3614 Jackson Highway, Sheffield, Alabama. The cause of their departure was, as ever, to do with money.

Rick Hall had signed a new deal with Capitol Records, that was rumoured to be worth $1,000,000. He then offered the musicians $10,000 each, according to Johnson. In the meantime, Jerry Wexler offered them eighteen months support and a $19,000 loan from Atlantic Records, to set up a new studio. It was a gamble, of course, but they decided to take it.

It was an attractive offer. Wexler was offering the four musicians the chance to own and run their own studio and the loan made that more achievable. He had also demonstrated in the past his admiration for their work, when he called them to New York to finish Aretha Franklin's aborted FAME sessions. It seemed that they would be able to continue working with major Atlantic Records artists, whilst building up their own contacts. The opportunity to make more money, while taking control of their working lives, was too good to miss.

Key musicians from the first FAME session band had moved to Nashville for very similar reasons, and now Rick Hall was faced with history repeating itself, with the added problem that the four key members of the second session band were now going to be nearby, in a new studio. He must have wondered if Jerry Wexler was still trying to teach him a lesson, after the dispute during Aretha's Franklin's session, and he was clearly angry with the four musicians for leaving so suddenly. For a while he felt betrayed, but he also realised pretty quickly that he had contributed to the problem.

He later acknowledged that his management of the situation had not been good enough: "I should have gone partners with them or cut them in for a piece of the action, but I think I had really come to believe that I could take any group of musicians and cut hit records. I just wasn't smart enough, or I was too engrossed in what I was doing, to realise differently." (See Paul McGuinness' article on the udiscovermusic website, April 27th, 2021).

Hall's solution to the problems posed by the departure of the quartet was to put together a new band made up of people he had already worked with and other musicians who came highly recommended. The hand-over was quickly achieved, with new members of band picking up all the unfinished work.

Hall called his new session band the FAME Gang, which consisted of a four-piece rhythm section and a four-piece horn section, with a mixture of Black and White musicians.

17

Junior Lowe

Albert "Junior" Lowe was born in Florence in 1940 and got his first guitar at the age of six. Six years later, he put a band together and started playing seriously. His main interests were Country and Gospel music. He later played guitar with the Fairlanes, replacing Rick Hall as the group's bass player when Rick left the group to develop FAME.

He went on to play many sessions for Rick Hall at FAME and Quin Ivy at Norala. He was an obvious choice to take over from Jimmy Johnson and David Hood, as he played lead guitar and bass and knew the studio well.

Jesse Boyce

Jesse Boyce was born in North Carolina in 1948. He was a classically trained musician, who learned to play piano, organ, drums, bass and guitar. He completed his degree at American Baptist College in Nashville and went on to join the third FAME Studios session band, playing mainly bass.

At FAME, he worked on sessions with Clarence Carter, Candi Staton, Wilson Pickett and many other singers. He later formed several groups, often in collaboration with Moses Dillard, and worked and recorded in Nashville. He was an accomplished songwriter, providing songs for many well-known artists, including Linda Clifford, the Temptations, Ben E. King, the Dells and the Commodores.

From the mid-eighties, he worked for around thirty years as a member of Little Richard's band. He died in 2016.

Clayton Ivey

Herbert Clayton Ivey was born in Pensacola, Florida, where he learned to play keyboards. He often played with Jesse Boyce. In 1969 he joined FAME, along with Boyce. One of their first sessions was with Clarence Carter, for the recording of "Patches". After that, Clayton was committed to a career in music. He stayed at FAME for a couple years, working on the Osmonds' sessions, before working freelance.

In 1971 he set up a music production company called Wishbone Productions with Terry Woodford, a musician and songwriter. They established a roster of young artists and helped them get established. They also signed a contract with Motown in 1973, to work with some of their young artists, in particular Reuben Howell.

Ivey was invited to join the band at the Muscle Shoals Sound Studio for various sessions, which gave him the opportunity to work with Lulu, Rod Stewart and other artists.

In 1976, the deal with Motown came to an end and Wishbone Productions opened its own studio on Webster Avenue in Muscle Shoals, with the latest technology, including 24-track recording equipment.

In May 2021, Clayton Ivey gave an interview to the Musicians Hall of Fame, in which he speaks of his excitement as a young musician making his way to FAME Studios and working with the FAME Gang. He describes how the songs were often made by a process of collaboration between the songwriters and the session band, working things out by experiment. They had a focus that made good things happen and they were willing to work for as long as it took to get a song to work.

The excitement of that process was a feature of sessions not just at FAME, but at many of the studios in New Orleans, Memphis, Detroit and Chicago. It is a process that is enhanced by the creation of a strong session band, whose members grow together. That experience is what Ivey remembers most about his early days in the music business.

Freeman Brown

When the Swampers left FAME in 1969, Rick Hall began using various drummers. Some were independent, like Fred Pouty, who played on some of the Osmonds' hits, James Stroud and Owen Hale. A few others like Freeman Brown were signed to FAME. Brown played on Clarence Carter's 1969 album "Testifyin'", completing the work that had been started by Roger Hawkins.

Rick Hall described Brown as "steady as a rock". Wilson Pickett highlighted the precision of his playing: "He wasn't all over the drums on recordings, but he was always just there."

Freeman Brown died in 2017 at the age of seventy-four.

FAME Studios 2013

Photo: Ralph Daily (Wikimedia Commons)

Roger Clark

Rick Hall later signed a young drummer from Chatanooga, Tennessee, Roger Clark, who had played his first gig aged just fourteen. He had gained a lot of experience playing as a member of Steve Miller's touring band and had also done some studio work on the West Coast, before an old friend suggested he should go to FAME. Clark played on Clarence Carter's 1973 album "Sixty Minutes With Clarence Carter", going on to contribute to a large number of the hits made at FAME during the seventies.

Rick Hall rated Clark very highly: "Roger was a wonderful player with a touch and feel like no other drummer I ever used. You will hear an example of this when you hear his playing on "Baby, Baby Don't Get Hooked on Me," which became a number-one record for Mac Davis." (See the *Modern Drummer* website).

Clark also worked on sessions at Wishbone Productions' studio in Muscle Shoals, including a track called "Guilty" for the band HOT, which achieved gold accreditation. Clark also had a writing credit for the song.

He was invited to play on some sessions at Motown along with Clayton Ivey. Amongst the collection of gold and platinum discs that he accumulated is "Firefly", a song he recorded with the Temptations.

Clark's work at Wishbone with Hank Williams Jr. led to an invitation from Nashville producer Jimmy Bowen to go to work there with the Elektra/Asylum roster of artists. More hits followed with some of Elektra's Country music stars.

Roger Clark died in 2018 at his home on Wilson Lake, part of the Tennessee River in the Shoals area.

Mickey Buckins

Charles Michael Buckins was a local Muscle Shoals singer, who led his own band, Mickey Buckins and the New Breed, in the mid-sixties. In 1965, Buckins recorded a single entitled "Silly Girl" at Norala Studios with Quin Ivy, probably with the support of the Mosriters. It didn't sell well, but he went on to record two more singles on Ivy's South Camp label, "Seventeen Year Old Girl" (B-side "Long Long Time"), produced by Marlin Greene and Eddie Hinton, and "Reflections of Charles Brown" (B-side "Big Boy Pete"), produced by Quin Ivy.

Possibly attracted by his songwriting skills, Rick Hall offered Buckins a job at FAME in 1967. Hall needed to replace Dan Penn, who had left to join Chips Moman in Memphis, and Buckins could fill that slot. Penn had also been heavily involved in producing and sound-engineering, working alongside Hall, and now Hall set about training Buckins to fill that role too. Buckins learned quickly and rose through the ranks, moving from assistant to chief engineer, becoming a producer and studio manager. He also took part in recording sessions, playing percussion. Just as Penn had done, he became Hall's right-hand man.

For a short while Buckins moved to Memphis. In 1969, George Jackson persuaded Rick Hall to open a small studio in Memphis to record demo tracks for artists who were interested in possibly signing for FAME. Buckins was put in charge of the new venue. Unfortunately, Jackson's assessment of the number of talented local singers who were waiting to be given their chance at FAME was over-optimistic. The studio in Memphis was closed and Buckins returned to Muscle Shoals. In 1969 he engineered Solomon Burke's album "Proud Mary" at the FAME studios and produced the FAME Gang's single "Grits And Gravy".

Buckins also developed into an accomplished songwriter,

responsible for Janie Fricke's "Tell Me a Lie", which topped the charts. Other artists to record his songs are Clarence Carter, the Osmonds, Millie Jackson, Spencer Wiggins and Jason Isbell and Joss Stone.

Buckins has spent over fifty years working in the Muscle Shoals music industry!

Travis Wammack

The FAME Gang that took over session duties from the Swampers is generally regarded as a rhythm section group of four men, plus the Muscle Shoals Horns, four horn players. However, the credits on albums produced at FAME Studios from 1969 onwards show that several more musicians were regularly involved in the sessions. One of these was guitarist Travis Wammack, born in Walnut, Mississippi, in 1946. He started out in the music business aged eleven, when he recorded one of his own songs, "Rock And Roll Blues"! His first chart entry was an instrumental called "Scratchy" in 1964.

Wammack worked as a session musician in Memphis from 1961, which brought him to the attention of Rick Hall. From 1968, Hall began calling on Wammack's services, for Clarence Carter's albums "Slippin' Around" (1968), "Willie And Laura Mae Jones" (1970), and "Patches" (also 1970). He later recorded with Bobbie Gentry, the Osmonds, Wilson Pickett, Aretha Franklin, Mac Davis, Lou Rawls, Candi Staton, Percy Sledge and many more.

Rick Hall signed him to the FAME label, releasing four singles and an album "Travis Wammack", between 1972 and 1974. Wammack went on to lead Little Richard's backing band from 1984 to 1995. He is still performing and works at Muscle Shoals Music Marketing.

Duane Allman

Around the time Travis Wammack was beginning to work at FAME, another budding guitarist came to the studio. Duane Allman and his brother Gregg started to play guitar in 1960, while staying with their grandmother in Nashville during the summer. The boys were inspired to play Blues, when they saw B.B. King in concert in the city.

Duane's first venture into the professional music world came in 1966, when he was hired by producer Tony Moon to play some sessions at RCA's Studio B in Nashville. The two brothers then formed a band called the Allman Joys, playing regularly at the Briar Patch in Nashville, before reforming as Hour Glass.

In early 1968, Hour Glass came to FAME Studios to record. Rick Hall saw Duane's potential immediately and bought out his contract, putting him to work in the studio with Wilson Pickett. Duane camped out in the studio car park! During a break in one of the sessions, Duane played the Beatles' song "Hey Jude" to Pickett, and the decision was taken to record it. It became the title track of the subsequent album and, famously, brought Allman to the attention of Eric Clapton and Jerry Wexler. Rick Hall played it to Wexler over the 'phone and Wexler soon bought out the FAME contract!

Allman stayed in Muscle Shoals long enough to play on sessions with Clarence Carter, Aretha Franklin (in New York), King Curtis, Percy Sledge and several other performers outside the R&B field, before forming the Allman Brothers Band in 1969. Auditions for the band were held at FAME Studios.

Duane was a rising star in the world of Blues music, playing on Eric Clapton's "Layla and Other Assorted Love Songs", released as a Derek and the Dominos album in 1970. At the age of twenty-four, Duane was killed in a motorcycle accident in 1971.

Recommended Track:

1968 Wilson Pickett: "Hey Jude"

The FAME Gang released an album and a couple of singles in their own name, starting with a single "Spooky", released on Atlantic Records in 1968. That was followed by a second single "Grits And Gravy" (B-side "Soul Feud") on the FAME label in 1969. They then released an album called "Solid Gold From Muscle Shoals", which failed to make any impact. It was a collection of instrumental covers of songs that had recently been in the charts, but it didn't do justice to the quality of their session work. In 1970 a third single "Twangin' My Thang" was released, again on FAME, produced by Mickey Buckins.

"Grits & Gravy", the 2015 FAME Gang album

(used with permission of Ace Records UK)

The best of their work as a band can be heard on a compilation album that was released in 2015 on Ace Records'

BGP label, called "Grits & Gravy: The Best of the FAME Gang". It contains a selection of songs from the earlier album and the singles, plus a lot of new material from the vaults at FAME.

From 1972, some new musicians were brought in regularly to work with Clarence Carter, Candi Staton, Z.Z. Hill and others. Ken Bell (guitar) and Tim Henson (keyboards) were amongst them.

New Songwriters at FAME

In addition to the musicians, of course, Rick Hall was keen to attract good songwriters to FAME. He had lost his two best songwriters, Dan Penn in 1967 and Spooner Oldham in 1968. Both had gone to work in Memphis with Chips Moman at American Sound Studios.

At the end of the sixties, Hall hired two new songwriters. George Jackson was from Mississippi but, as a guitar-playing singer songwriter, he toured widely in the Southern States during the sixties and knew Memphis well. Raymond Moore was a native of Memphis. They often worked together at FAME.

George Jackson started out as a singer, working with Ike Turner before going to Memphis, where he joined Louis Williams in setting up the Ovations at Goldwax Records. He wrote songs for several of the Goldwax artists. After a brief stop at Hi Records, Jackson took up a suggestion from Billy Sherrill, who had helped Rick Hall set up FAME, and came to Muscle Shoals to work. His early successes as a FAME songwriter included "Too Weak To Fight" for Clarence Carter in 1968 and "I'd Rather Be An Old Man's Sweetheart" for Candi Staton in 1969, which he wrote with Clarence Carter and Raymond Moore. Jackson's biggest success came in 1971, when the Osmonds came to FAME and picked one of Jackson's songs for their first FAME release. "One Bad Apple" went to number one on the Pop chart. Jackson left FAME in 1972, moving to Muscle Shoals Sound Studios.

Altogether Jackson amassed 782 credits for songwriting and arranging before his death in 2013. He also released a number of singles on a variety of labels, including two at FAME, "Find 'Em, Fool 'Em And Forget 'Em" in 1969 and "That's How Much You Mean To Me" in 1970. Jackson actually recorded over a hundred songs at FAME, but they were demos, used by Rick Hall, when visiting artists came to record. They were proper recordings, if occasionally stripped back, that were not intended for release. They just stayed in the vaults at FAME, ready to be picked up whenever they were needed. Ace Records managed to unlock them fifty years after they were made, subsequently issuing five George Jackson at FAME albums on their Kent imprint, alongside a compilation of Jackson's Goldwax songs and another Memphis compilation. In 2002 and 2005, two compilations of Jackson's Muscle Shoals Sound songs were released by Grapevine in the UK, recorded with the Swampers.

After years of waiting, this collection of albums, containing many of his best songs, gives a real insight into just how important Jackson was to the development of Southern Soul.

George Jackson's album "Don't Count Me Out" on Kent Records

(used with permission of Ace Records UK)

Raymond Moore

Raymond Moore began writing songs as a young man in Memphis. Some of his early compositions were recorded by Rufus and Carla Thomas and Sam & Dave. In the late sixties he came to FAME, where he wrote for Clarence Carter, Candi Staton, Wilson Pickett, and Bobbie Gentry. Moore and Jackson co-wrote "Poor Man" for Willie Hightower, and "Whatever Turns You On" for Travis Wammack. In 1972, he left FAME with George Jackson, moving to Muscle Shoals Sound Studios. He is credited with over 350 songs, some co-written, which is some achievement, when you consider that he also held down a job in Memphis through his songwriting years.

18
THE MUSCLE SHOALS HORNS

In 1967 Rick Hall decided to set up a horn section at FAME Studios, probably influenced by the success of the Memphis Horns, Wayne Jackson and Andrew Love. He had been hiring the Memphis Horns for studio work at FAME, but the cost of bringing them in from Memphis suggested that a FAME horn section might be more cost-effective.

FAME Studio A (2010)

Photo: Carol M. Highsmith (Library of Congress)

Wikimedia Commons

Most of the musicians to whom he offered contracts for the horn section were experienced in the field of Jazz and had received formal music training. The line-up remained together (with one change) until the mid-eighties, working at FAME and at other studios in the Shoals area. Four men formed the core of the horn section, augmented as necessary by other session musicians. The four were Ronnie Eades, Aaron Varnell, Harrison Calloway and Harvey Thompson. In 1970, Varnell left and was later replaced by Charles Rose. When those first contracts expired, the group decided to go freelance, calling themselves the Muscle Shoal Horns. They were then able to take work not just at FAME Studios but also at other studios in the wider Shoals area and beyond.

Calloway, Eades and Thompson met each other as students whilst at Tennessee State University in Nashville. They started performing together, supporting various local bands, and on one occasion played with a young guitarist called Jimi Hendrix!

Eades later crossed paths with Barry Beckett, a fellow native of Birmingham, Alabama. They were both in Pensacola, Florida, working with Don Schroeder, when the opportunity arose to join a recording session at FAME Studios that Schroeder organized for James and Bobby Purify.

From 1967 onwards, members of the new horn section became members of the new FAME Gang and played on some classic albums recorded at FAME, including recordings by Clarence Carter, Candi Staton, Wilson Pickett and Etta James.

Later, they released several albums under the Muscle Shoals Horns name: "Born To Get Down" (1976), "Doin' It To The Bone" (1977) and "Shine On" (1983).

In 2015, after a gap of thirty years, they played together once more, to celebrate the re-release of their albums as CDs.

In 2019, the original Muscle Shoals Horns were inducted into the Musicians Hall of Fame and Museum in Nashville.

Ronnie Eades

Ronnie Eades was born in Tarrant City, Alabama, near Birmingham, in 1942. At the age of ten he started playing saxophone and also took oboe lessons. He played with a variety of groups, including the Esquires. In 1966, he came to FAME with Don Shroeder and Barry Beckett to work on "I'm Your Puppet" with James and Bobby Purify. Barry Beckett contacted him the following year to tell him that Rick Hall was setting up a horn section. Eades decided to move to the Muscle Shoals area to seek work at FAME.

When he found out that Hall was looking for a baritone sax player, Eades bought one and offered his services. The investment paid off! He signed a contract with FAME Studios in 1967 and joined the FAME Gang. One of the first sessions he worked on was Clarence Carter's "Patches".

Eades did not have the formal training that some of his fellow musicians had, but he was a quick learner and picked up what he needed from those around him. The most important lesson of all he learned from Rick Hall, as he explained in an interview with David Blacker for airgigs.com: "Rick taught us that session musicians had to be very creative". He learned to keep things simple, to enhance the song, rather than clash with the artist's vision. "Never take away from what the artist is doing".

By 1981, Eades had played with over four hundred different singers.

Harrison Calloway

Harrison Calloway was born in Chattanooga, Tennessee, in 1941. He teamed up with Ronnie Eades and Harvey Thompson while at university in Nashville, playing trumpet, and joined them at FAME in 1969. He also played flugelhorn and piano.

He became the unofficial leader of the horn section, contributing many key ideas to the sessions. He worked with all the FAME artists and then, when the Muscle Shoals Horns went freelance, with the Osmonds, Bob Seger, Bob Dylan, Elton John and many others.

He developed into a songwriter, producer and arranger, as well as trumpet player. Later in his career he worked at Malaco Records in Jackson, Mississippi.

Harrison Calloway died in Jackson in 2016.

Harvey Thompson

Harvey Thompson went to school in Tuscalosa, Alabama, and later studied music at Tennessee State University. He started playing with Eades and Calloway while still a student. Local Nashville R&B singers used to come to the campus to find students willing to play for them. It was an excellent introduction to the music business. Rick Hall signed all three to the FAME Gang, taking advantage of their musical capabilities and their experience of playing together. Thompson's first recordings at FAME Studios were the Muscle Shoals Horns album in 1969 and Clarence Carter's "Patches" album, released in 1970. He played tenor sax and flute, contributing to hundreds of sessions. His credits include recordings with Candi Staton, Joe Tex, Bobby Womack and many more.

As a member of the Muscle Shoals Horns, he played on sessions at other local studios, including Muscle Shoals Sound Studios and at Malaco Records. It was at Malaco that the horn section joined the sessions for Dorothy Moore's "Misty Blue" album, released in 1976.

Later in his career, Thompson toured with Lyle Lovett and

played with a diverse group of artists, including John Denver, Elton John and Kim Carnes.

A recent session at NuttHouse Recording Studio in Muscle Shoals (July 2018) illustrated another side of Thompson's musical interests. It was a live recording of an album entitled "Muscle Shoals Jazz", played by the Harvey Thompson Trio and released on Crazy Chester Records. The "trio" consists of Harvey, his son Harvey Jr. on electric piano, Phil Lee on bass guitar and Marcus Pope on drums. It was this versatility that persuaded Rick Hall to hire those young horn players from Tennessee State University.

Aaron Varnell

Aaron Varnell joined the FAME Gang as a trombone player. He played on sessions in 1968 with Clarence Carter and Etta James, in 1969 with Wilson Pickett, in 1970 with Clarence Carter for the "Patches" album, and in 1971 with Candi Staton for the "Stand By Your Man" sessions. He left FAME at the end of 1971 and was replaced by Charles Rose.

Charles Rose

Charles Rose is a native of Sheffield, Alabama. He studied music at Murray State University, majoring in trombone. He also plays keyboards, arranges and produces. In recent years he has been leader of the Muscle Shoals Horns and of his own Jazz combo, the Charlie Rose Trio (on piano!).

His contributions at FAME started in 1971. Since then, he has played on hundreds of sessions, covering a wide range of musical styles.

19
SOLOMON BURKE

Up until 1967, Rick Hall relied mainly on artists he signed to FAME Records, plus artists signed to Atlantic Records, brought to the Shoals by Jerry Wexler, to fill the bulk of the studio time. When Wexler withdrew his artists following the altercation with Rick Hall over the behaviour of one of the FAME session band, Hall had to change the formula.

Clarence Carter and Candi Staton were the two mainstays of the next few years, singers on whom Hall could build the FAME brand. But he needed more. The answer was to attract visitors such as Etta James and Solomon Burke, both of whom had a strong profile in the music industry and could therefore add to FAME's reputation.

Solomon Burke 1967

Atlantic Records Trade Ad (Wikimedia Commons)

Solomon Burke had signed to Atlantic Records in 1960 and had benefitted from working with Jerry Wexler. He recorded thirty-two singles, most of which had entered the Pop and R&B charts and had achieved two big R&B hits in 1965 with "Got to Get You Off My Mind", which went to number one, and "Tonight's the Night", which reached number two. In subsequent years, the successes tailed off, as Wilson Pickett and Aretha Franklin became the big R&B stars at Atlantic.

Wexler did not bring Solomon Burke to Muscle Shoals, as he did Pickett and Franklin. Instead, Burke took the initiative and went to Chips Moman's American Sound Studio in Memphis in search of inspiration. He later decided to leave Atlantic and join Bell Records, working with his new manager Tamiko Jones, whom he met at American Sound.

Together they came to FAME Studios in 1969 to record an album, which they co-produced, called "Proud Mary". The selection of songs for the album covers a range of styles and sources, but there are three tracks from local songwriters, with a Muscle Shoals signature sound. The opening track is a John Fogerty song "Proud Mary", which Creedence Clearwater Revival had released in 1968. It features a strong horn section, playing Memphis style. Track two is the Otis Redding song "These Arms of Mine" from 1962, sung in a similar style to Otis, backed by melodic horns and organ in typical Muscle Shoals fashion. That is followed by "I'll Be Doggone", written by Marv Tarlin, Warren Moore and Smokey Robinson at Motown and released by Marvin Gaye in 1965. Burke's version features a country-style guitar line a touch of harmonica, which are more Nashville than Detroit. Solomon Burke was clearly not afraid to follow in the footsteps of some great singers!

Track four, "How Big A Fool (Can A Fool Be), is a song written by Solomon Burke himself, with strong echoes of Motown. Side A is completed by "Don't Wait Too Long", a song written by FAME's Mickey Buckins, who was sound engineer on the album. Buckins' inspiration was probably Otis Redding; the song is a Soul classic, which shows the power of Burke's voice.

The B-side combines two songs by FAME songwriters with some older songs. "That Lucky Old Sun" is a ballad written by Beasley Smith and Haven Gillespie in 1949, given the Solomon Burke power treatment. The next two tracks are home-grown. "Uptight Good Woman", written by Dan Penn, Spooner Oldham and Jimmy Johnson, and "I Can't Stop (No, No, No), written by Dan Penn and Roger Hawkins, are typical FAME songs, one slow and one up-tempo. The first was recorded in 1967 by Wilson Pickett. The second was recorded by Arthur Conley in 1966. They are two more classics of the Muscle Shoals sound.

"Please Send Me Someone to Love" is a slow Blues ballad first recorded by Percy Mayfield in 1950, released on Specialty Records. It went to number one on the R&B chart. The final song is "What Am I Living For", written by Fred Jay and Art Harris, which also went to number one on the R&B chart in 1958, sung by Chuck Willis. Ernest Tubb released a Country version of the song in 1959, followed by a Pop version from Conway Twitty in 1960. The song acquired some R&B pedigree in 1967, when Percy Sledge recorded his version, probably the inspiration for Solomon Burke.

In an interview with Roger Catlin in the Hartford Courant in 1996, Burke described how he first used the term Soul music. A journalist had asked him what kind of singer he wanted to be. Burke's answer was: "I want to be a soul singer". He wanted his music to be inspirational and gospel based. Given his background in the church, that was understandable. Many people in the church regarded Blues and R&B as the music of the Devil, and Burke wasn't the first to face this problem. Sam Cooke and Aretha Franklin had similar misgivings about getting involved in secular music. For all three, and many others, the solution was to sing from the soul.

Solomon Burke never attained the heights achieved by Sam Cooke and Aretha Franklin, but he was a prolific and influential talent. His recording at FAME Studios is a powerful addition to the FAME discography, highlighting the musical abilities of the FAME session men and demonstrating to many other artists that a visit to Muscle Shoals could bring rewards.

Solomon Burke 2008

Photo: Tom Beetz (Wikimedia Commons)

Three singles were released from the album, all of which entered the American Charts. In February 1969 "Uptight Good Woman" reached number one hundred and sixteen on the Pop chart and number forty-seven on the R&B chart. In May, "Proud Mary" did better, rising to number forty-five Pop and number fifteen R&B. Finally in July, "That Lucky Old Sun" went to number one hundred and twenty-nine on the Pop chart.

Recommended Tracks:

1969 Solomon Burke: "Don't Wait Too Long"

1969 Solomon Burke: "Uptight Good Woman"

20

The amazing output from FAME Studios during the late sixties continued to attract new R&B artists to Rick Hall's studio. The transition from the Swampers to the FAME Gang was completed in 1969 and Hall made an important decision to widen the range of artists who might be tempted to visit. He was still keen to work with Black R&B singers, but he realized that the competition had intensified. His old session band, with support from Jerry Wexler, soon set up their own studio in the Shoals area in direct competition with FAME. Hall therefore had to widen the scope of FAME's output and search further afield for artists, both Black and White, covering a wider range of genres, including Pop and Country, as well as R&B. It was a new era at FAME and success was by no means guaranteed. The big names had nearly all gone elsewhere.

Many of the artists who came to FAME Studios in search of success were talented and determined, but somehow many of them failed to make the impact that the record companies were looking for. They moved on, tried again somewhere else, and sometimes they found the missing ingredients. For others, the disappointment was too strong, and they gave up their dreams of becoming icons in the music industry.

Nevertheless, the work of these lesser-known artists is often worth a listen. The songs are good and there are hidden gems waiting to be found in the vaults of most record companies. Here are some of the artists who recorded at FAME without achieving any big hits.

Lou Johnson came to FAME Studios in 1969 to record his first album. That makes him sound like a beginner, but he had signed for Bigtop Records in New York in 1962. He had recorded a number of singles that made the charts, thanks to the song-writing skills of Hal David and Burt Bacharach, but he came to FAME in search of a major breakthrough. In 1968 he had signed to Cotillion Records, an Atlantic Records subsidiary label, with Jerry Wexler, Tom Dowd and Arif Mardin directing him for the sessions in Alabama. This was his big opportunity.

Unfortunately, the choice of songs was not strong. Only two were original, both written by Don Covay. The album "Sweet Southern Soul" failed to make much impact. The three singles taken from the album, released in 1968 and 1969, all failed to chart.

A second album, "With You In Mind", was recorded in New Orleans, with Allen Toussaint at the helm, released on the Stax/Volt label. When that also yielded no hits, Johnson moved to California and earned his living as a club singer. He died in 2019. Several of his songs subsequently became popular on the Northern Soul circuit in the UK: "Magic Potion" and "Unsatisfied" are the two best.

Recommended Track:

1969 Lou Johnson: "She Thinks I Still Care"

James Govan was born in Mississippi but moved to Memphis as a child. It was in Memphis that one of FAME's songwriters George Jackson first heard Govan singing. On Jackson's recommendation, Govan was signed to FAME Records. Jackson introduced Govan to Mickey Buckins, who took him to FAME in 1969, where he recorded "Wanted: Lover", a song previously recorded there by Laura Lee in 1967. When the single failed to sell, Buckins came up with a new idea. He suggested Govan sing some contemporary pop songs, adding a typical FAME slant, plus some songs written by the FAME team. Altogether, the FAME sessions generated sixteen tracks. One of the pop songs and one of the FAME songs were chosen as the next single, George Harrison's "Something" and a George Jackson/ Mickey Buckins composition entitled "You Get A Lot To Like", released in 1970.

Just as Chess Records had left many of the FAME recordings in the vaults, so Rick Hall now did the same with the James Govan material. And just as with Chess, it took the efforts of Ace Records in the UK to bring them back into the light of day. Ace released a retrospective Govan album in 2013, giving it a title that echoed the first single, "Wanted: The FAME Recordings", on their Kent label.

James Govan's album "Wanted: The FAME Recordings" on Kent Records

(used with permission of Ace Records UK)

The album has a lot of merit, and the sixteen tracks show why several people in the music business saw Govan as the next Otis Redding. FAME Records released their own retrospective compilation in 2019, "The FAME Recordings", with twelve of the sixteen tracks.

The collection of songs is unusual, combining some Muscle Shoals compositions with covers of a variety of well-known Pop songs, albeit written by master songwriters Lennon and McCartney, Carole King and Bob Dylan.

Sadly, Buckins' idea didn't work in terms of sales. Govan left FAME and went back to Memphis. But he was not quite finished with Muscle Shoals. In 1983 he came back, not to FAME but to Broadway Sound studio in Sheffield, where he recorded his first album. Broadway was originally Quinvy Studios, built by Quin Ivy around 1968, but it now belonged to David Johnson, Ivy's former engineer, who produced the album. The session band was exceptional! David Hood (bass), Roger Hawkins (drums) and Jimmy Johnson (guitar) came over from Muscle Shoals Sound Studio. The Muscle Shoals horns turned up too, Harrison Calloway Jr. (Trumpet), Ronnie Eades (baritone sax), Charles Rose (trombone) and Harvey Thompson (tenor sax). Clayton Ivey (keyboards), Roger Clark (drums) and Travis Wammack (guitar) all added contributions. The album, entitled "I'm In Need", appeared in 1987 on Charly Records, re-released in 1996 by Over-Eazy/Overture Music. Charly issued it again in 2013. Finally, in 2014, David Johson released his own version of the same songs, giving the album a much better name: "The Muscle Shoals Recordings". So, after waiting years to hear most of James Govan's recordings, fans now have access to twenty-five studio tracks, plus a live album or two.

The best of the songs are slow ballads, often with an Otis Redding style phrasing. George Jackson wrote many of them. The quality of the recordings is excellent, both at FAME and at Broadway, with Govan's powerful voice always to the fore. The Broadway songs often have excellent backing vocals and a strong horn arrangement. Amongst the more up-tempo tracks are "Stuck On You", with its bouncy Sam & Dave beat, and a cover of Elvis Presley's "That's Alright Mama" (written by Arthur "Big Boy" Crudup). Another cover hints at the Country music links between Muscle Shoals and Nashville: "Waylon Jennings' song "We had It All" becomes a powerful Soul ballad in the hands of James Govan. Perhaps the most surprising choice of all was "Way Over Yonder", a lovely Carole King song, that Govan delivers with intimacy and passion, with a strong Gospel feel.

Later Govan teamed up with another local musician Don Chandler and, together with the Boogie Blues Band, took up a residency at the Rum Boogie Café on Beale Street, which lasted from 1989 until 2014, when Govan died.

He was a talented singer, who somehow never got lucky. His songs have certainly stood the test of time and are well worth seeking out.

Recommended Tracks: (both tracks recorded in 1969)

2013 James Govan: "I Shall Be Released"

2013 James Govan: "Way Over Yonder"

Spencer Wiggins

Spencer Wiggins was born in Memphis, in the same part of town as James Carr and Bobby Bland. He grew up singing Gospel music, forming a Gospel group whilst still at school, with his brother Percy and sister Maxine. After leaving Booker T. Washington High School, he formed a group to sing R&B songs, that included Percy once more and David Porter, who later went on to be a leading songwriter at Stax Records.

In the early sixties Wiggins joined Goldwax records but failed to find success. His first contact with Rick Hall came later in the sixties, when, like several of the Goldwax artists, he came to FAME Studios to record several singles, including a version of "I Never Loved A Woman (The Way I Loved You)", featuring Duane Allman on guitar. When Goldwax closed down in 1969, Wiggins signed for FAME Records. Rick Hall bought several tracks that had been recorded but not yet released, including "Love Machine"/ "Love Me Tonight", which failed to chart when issued by FAME. He had better luck in 1970, when his follow-up release "Double Lovin'"/ "I'd Rather Go Blind" reached number forty-four on the Billboard R&B chart.

With no more success on the horizon, Wiggins moved to Florida, where he became active in the Baptist church, releasing an album of Gospel songs in 2003.

The 2010 album "Feed the Flame" on Kent Records

(used with permission of Ace Records UK)

Once more, the record companies involved stored all Wiggins' recordings in their vaults for many years, until they were brought to light on a series of compilations put together by Japanese and UK companies, Vivid Sound and Ace Records (on the Kent label). All the tracks that Wiggins recorded at FAME are available on the Ace Records compilation "Feed The Flame: The FAME and XL Recordings", released on the Kent label in 2010.

Recommended Tracks: (both recorded in 1969)

2010 Spencer Wiggins: "Cry To Me"

2010 Spencer Wiggins: "I Never Loved A Woman (The Way I Loved You)"

Willie Hightower

Willie Hightower was born in Gadsden, Alabama, in 1940. He started singing in church choirs aged six and later joined Gospel groups. Inspired by meeting Sam Cooke, when he came to perform in Gadsden, Hightower formed an R&B group and in 1965 recorded his first secular song "What Am I Living For" for Bobby Robinson's Enjoy label in New York. Later singles were released on the Fury label, with a switch in 1967 to Capitol Records, with several of them recorded in Memphis. His first chart entry came in 1968 with "It's a Miracle", a song that he had written with producer Bobby Robinson.

It was the link with Capitol Records that brought Willie Hightower to FAME studios in 1970 to record a cover of Joe South's "Walk a Mile in My Shoes" with Rick Hall producing. Hall suggested the song and, unsurprisingly, given his track record, it was Hightower's second hit, reaching number twenty-six R&B and number one hundred and seven on the Pop chart. The B-side was "You Used Me Baby", a song that Hightower had co-written with his grandmother! The FAME Gang played on both tracks.

Hightower went on to release two more singles on the FAME label. "Time Has Brought About a Change" (1970) was inspired by Sam Cooke. It is a powerful, emotional song, with string arrangements by Jimmy Haskell and horn arrangements by Harrison Calloway. The B-side is a lighter ballad written by George Jackson and Mickey Buckins entitled "I Can't Love Without You".

The final single release was O.B. Clinton's song "Back Road into Town" (1971), which took Hightower into Clarence Carter territory. The B-side, "Poor Man", also has a Country-Soul feel. These tracks are all well-written songs, with strong arrangements and excellent backing from the FAME Gang. Unfortunately, the second and third singles failed to sell well, leading Rick Hall to conclude that the album that he had been contemplating would probably not succeed either. The idea was dropped, and Hightower moved on.

He made several more singles but soon relied on live performances to earn his living.

Out of the blue, Hightower re-emerged in 1982, when he received a telephone call from Quinton Claunch at his home in Gadsden, inviting him to record an album in Memphis with Willie Mitchell at Royal Studios. The sessions were spread over two days, producing twelve songs, with an excellent session band of Teenie Hodges (guitar), Leroy Hodges (bass), Charles Hodges (keyboards), Howard Grimes (drums), Andrew Love (tenor sax), James Mitchell (baritone sax) and Gene Miller (trumpet).

For many years, the rest of his music was largely unavailable, until, in 2004, Honest Jon Records in the UK issued a compilation "Willie Hightower", which triggered a lot of interest amongst fans of Northern Soul. Eight years later Capitol Records issued their version of the album, which included the tracks recorded at FAME. In 2016, Capital re-issued Hightower's pre-FAME album "If I Had a Hammer", with the FAME songs added as bonus tracks.

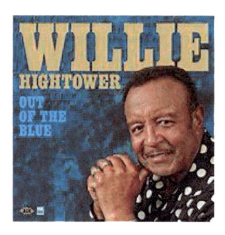

The 2018 album "Out of the Blue" on Ace Records

(used with permission of Ace Records UK)

These compilations rekindled interest in Hightower and Quinton Claunch stepped in once again in 2015, to offer Hightower the opportunity to record some new songs, at the age of seventy-seven, back in Muscle Shoals!

The recordings took place at a new studio in the Shoals called Big Star Studio, which was owned by Billy Lawson, the former sound engineer at Wishbone Studios. Altogether they recorded ten songs and Claunch began to look for a distributor.

That process took some time, but eventually the album, entitled "Out Of The Blue" was issued by Ace Records in the UK in 2018. The songs are smooth Soul ballads, with Hightower's voice still in good shape. He may not be an icon, but Hightower never stopped trying.

Recommended Tracks:

1970 Willie Hightower: "Walk A Mile In My Shoes"

1970 Willie Hightower: "Time Has Brought About A Change"

1971 Willie Hightower: "Back Road Into Town"

Bettye Swann

Bettye Jean Champion was born in Shreveport, Louisiana, in 1944, one of fourteen children. Her family were sharecroppers.

She grew up listening to Sam Cooke and sang in her school choir. At the age of eighteen, she left Louisiana and went to Los Angeles to live with one of her sisters. She was a natural singer, whose voice was noticed. Eventually she came to the attention of Ruth Dolphin, owner of Money Records in L.A., with whom she made some recordings. It was at this point in 1964 that she adopted the stage name Bettye Swann.

She didn't have to wait long for her first hit, the appropriately named "Don't Wait Too Long", which she had written. It must have all seemed pretty easy, as it entered the R&B chart. In 1967, her future looked assured when her single "Make Me Yours" went to number one on the Billboard R&B chart and number twenty-one on the Pop chart.

1968 brought a change of manager, a move to Capitol Records and relocation to Georgia. She married her new manager, George Barton. The next hit came in 1969, a cover of Jean Seely's "Don't Touch Me", which reached number fourteen R&B and number thirty-eight Pop. Two years later, she made a series of recordings at FAME Studios with Rick Hall.

The first of these was "I'm Just Living a Lie", released on the FAME label in 1971. She then signed for Atlantic Records for the release of the other FAME Studios tracks, "Victim of a Foolish Heart", written by George Jackson and Mickey Buckins, and "Today I Started Loving You Again"/ "I'd Rather Go Blind".

The second of these entered the R&B top twenty in 1972. It was later covered by Joss Stone in the UK on her 2003 album "The Soul Sessions". The third single is a cover of Etta James' big hit, with an interesting choice on the other side. "Today I Started Loving You Again" is a Merle Haggard/Bonnie Owens song, which, in Bettye Swann's version, is barely recognisable. Bettye Swann speeds things up a little, adding warmth and exuberance to the slower, laid-back original. The arrangements of horns and strings are both strong, emphasizing the natural optimism in Swann's voice. The single was sympathetically produced by Rick Hall and Mickey Buckins, with the FAME Gang and the Muscle Shoals Horns playing on the session. It is an excellent example of the style that evolved at FAME, merging elements of Soul and Country music, taking the recordings to a much wider audience.

Swann later recorded again in Los Angeles, before moving to Las Vegas. Her last performance was in 1980. Now known as Bettye Barton, she gave up the music industry, started work as a teacher and became a Jehovah's Witness.

Recommended Tracks:

1971 Bettye Swann: "Victim Of A Foolish Heart"

1972 Bettye Swann: "Today I Started Loving You Again"

21

FAME STUDIOS IN THE MAINSTREAM

In the early seventies, as tastes changed, Rick Hall realised that he would have to move with the times. He continued to support Black R&B artists, especially Clarence Carter and Candi Staton, but also set out to attract more mainstream singers. The first group to arrive was the **Osmonds**, brought to FAME Studios by Mike Curb, a record producer who had helped them secure a contract with MGM Records.

Their first release on the label was "One Bad Apple" in 1970. The song, written by FAME's George Jackson, reached the top of the Billboard Hot 100 Singles Chart week-ending February 17th, 1971 (5 weeks), going gold in the process and giving the group their first million-selling record. The track also made it to the number one position on the RPM 100 Singles Chart in Canada week-ending February 27th, 1971 (2 weeks). The "Osmonds" album also charted on Billboard Magazine's Best-Selling Soul LPs. It was on this chart for 13 weeks and the top chart position for the album was number thirteen for two weeks in March 1971. The album earned a gold record certification on September 13th, 1971, from the RIAA.

The entire album was produced by Rick Hall at FAME Recording Studios. On side one and again on side two, there are songs written by some of Motown Records' most successful songwriters and music producers, such as Strong and Whitfield and Holland, Dozier and Holland, plus tracks written by Gamble and Huff, famous for being the architects of "The Sound of Philadelphia" (TSOP). Musicians and producer featured on the "Osmonds" album, from which the gold-certified single "One Bad Apple" was taken, were Bob Wray (bass), Fred L. Prouty (drums), Albert S. Lowe Jr. and Travis Wammack (guitar), Leo Leblanc (steel guitar), Clayton

Ivey (keyboards), with Rick Hall producer. The Muscle Shoals Horns also played on the sessions: Ronnie Eades (baritone sax), Harvey Thompson (tenor sax), Dale Quillen (trombone) with Harrison Calloway and Jack Peck (trumpet).

A second album entitled "Homemade" was also produced by Hall. It was warmly promoted in the Billboard Magazine of June 19th, 1971: "The Osmond's second LP for MGM, cut with producer Rick Hall in Muscle Shoals, is another dynamite commercial package and it includes their single smash 'Double Lovin'. Other cuts that will stir play and sales are the opener, A Taste of Honey, The Promised Land, and She Makes Me Warm. The group members are in top vocal form and Hall's production is super." Peter Carpenter was responsible for string arrangements, Harrison Calloway Jr. arranged the horn parts, and Rick Hall again produced the album. The studio album "Homemade" debuted on the Billboard Top 200 Albums Chart listing on June 26th and peaked at number twenty-two. Altogether, it was on the chart for thirty-four weeks. In 1972, the album received a gold-certified plaque from the RIAA on January 20th.

The following single released in 1971 was "Yo-Yo" which became another smash hit for the group and a gold-certified track according to the RIAA. The single was extracted from "The Osmonds Phase-III" album which was released in 1971. The single peaked at number three on the Billboard Hot 100 Singles Chart. The following year the album earned a gold record disc from the RIAA for over half a million copies sold in America. Another gold single was obtained by the group with the track "Down The Lazy River", taken from the same album, which was gold-certified by the RIAA on March 24th 1972. The Osmonds sold eleven million records by the end of 1971, including singles and studio albums.

Donny Osmond released several FAME-recorded solo albums which were all million sellers. The first album produced by Hall for Donny was entitled "The Donny Osmond Album". It was released by MGM Records in June 1971 and peaked at number thirteen on the Billboard Top 200 Albums Chart and received in the process a gold plaque for half a million units sold in America. The album features one Billy Sherrill and Rick Hall track called "Sweet & Innocent". That song peaked at number seven on the Billboard Hot 100 Singles Chart and subsequently received an RIAA gold certification on August 30th, 1971. The single helped to push the album to number thirteen on the Billboard Top 200 Albums Chart. Donny Osmond had further success in Canada by going to number two on the country's Pop albums chart listing. "Sweet & Innocent" features the brilliant strings and woodwind arrangements of Jimmy Haskell which give the song a special quality.

Later that same year during the month of October MGM Records released another solo album by Donny Osmond entitled "To You With Love". The following year the album received a gold disc on January 26th. The single "Go Away Little Girl" from the album went to number one on the Billboard Hot 100 Singles Chart week-ending September 11th in 1971 (3 weeks), becoming in the process another gold record for Donny Osmond. Hall was credited as both record producer and sound engineer on the project. He also produced another smash hit during this period, receiving a gold disc for the single "Hey Girl" on July 28th 1972 from the RIAA.

On the third studio album for Donny Osmond entitled "Portrait Of Donny", Hall only co-produced four out of the eleven tracks listed. These songs were "Hey Girl", "All I Have To Do Is Dream", "Hey There, Lonely Girl" and "Big Man". The recording project was another great success for Donny Osmond when it received a gold certified plaque on December 30th in 1972 from the RIAA. The album contained one best-selling single called "Puppy Love" which obtained a gold plaque on March 24th in 1972. The single peaked at number three on the Billboard Hot 100 Singles Chart. Overseas the song also performed extremely well by going to number one on the Canadian RPM Singles Chart on April 15th 1972 (3 weeks) and also to number one on the UK Official Singles Chart week-ending July 8th 1972 (5 weeks).

The final album that features songs produced by Rick Hall was the compilation album "My Best to You". This was Donny Osmond's first greatest hits album to become certified gold in America by the RIAA on September 14th 1973.

According to the FAME website, the Osmond Brothers returned to FAME in the 80's to do their first country record and had two hits from the Elektra album. Marie Osmond also returned to do some work in the 90's. In 2001 Marie's son Steven Craig came to Muscle Shoals for a little magic on his upcoming Def Jam release.

In the meantime, Hall had diversified his creative efforts into Country music and produced a dynamic breakthrough album for **Mac Davis** in 1972. Davis had started recording at FAME in 1971 and went on to complete a string of twelve albums there. He had four gold or platinum records produced by Rick Hall. Hits that came from these were: "Baby Don't Get Hooked On Me", "Stop and Smell The Roses", "Friend Woman Lover Wife", "Texas In My Rearview Mirror" and "Hooked on Music".

The singer-songwriter Mac Davis's third studio album called "Baby, Don't Get Hooked on Me" became a best-seller in North America. The album received a gold-certified disc on March 7th 1973 for half a million units sold and eventually obtained a platinum plaque from the RIAA on November 21st 1986 for selling over a million copies. The title single "Baby Don't Get Hooked On Me" was number one on two singles chart listings in North America, the Billboard Hot 100 Singles Chart week-ending September 23rd 1972 (3 weeks) and the Billboard Easy Listening Singles Chart week-ending 16th

September 1972 (3 weeks). It also peaked at the top of the RPM Country Tracks Singles Chart in Canada week-ending October 21st 1972 (1 week).

Mac Davis went on to have further success with Hall and his team at FAME Studios with a gold-certified album "Stop And Smell The Roses" released in 1974 on Colombia Records. This peaked at number two on the Billboard Top Country Albums Chart that year and received its gold award from the RIAA on September 23rd 1974. The final collaboration between Rick Hall and Mac Davis was the gold-certified album "All The Love In The World" which was originally released by Colombia Records in December 1974. The album achieved gold certification on May 21st 1976.

Legendary singer/songwriter **Paul Anka** signed with United Artists Records and came to FAME to record the following smashes: "One Man Woman", "One Hell of A Woman", "I Don't Like To Sleep Alone" and "You're Having My Baby". All were million sellers, with the latter selling five million. The first album produced by Hall was a great success, with the single "You're Having My Baby" going to number one on the Billboard Hot 100 singles Chart week-ending August 24th 1974 (3 weeks) and receiving gold certification in the process, for one million units sold, awarded by the RIAA. In 1975 Anka had another gold plaque for the album "Times of Your Life", also co-produced by Hall at FAME Studios. The title track "Times of Your Life" was number one on the Billboard Adult Contemporary Singles Chart week-ending January 3rd 1976 (1 week).

It was thanks to Paul Anka that **Odia Coates** came to FAME Studios. Anka had heard Coates singing on an album by the Edwin Hawkins Singers and approached her to sing with him on several of the FAME Studios recordings, including "You're Having My Baby". In 1975 Coates recorded a solo album at FAME, with Rick Hall producing. "Odia Coates" features quite a few Paul Anka songs, plus several written or co-written by George Jackson. Surprisingly, one of the stand-out tracks is a cover of an ELO song written by Jeff Lynne. Coates' dramatic vocals give the song a strong R&B feel. "Heaven And Hell" is a powerful ballad, with an echo of Aretha Franklin. It is an interesting album, reminiscent of earlier times. The recordings are excellent, and Odia Coates has a powerful voice perfectly suited to the dramatic ballads on the album.

Recommended Tracks:

1975 Odia Coates: "Heaven and Hell"

1975 Odia Coates: "The Woman's Song"

1975 Odia Coates: "Don't Leave Me In the Morning"

Rhodes, Chalmers, Rhodes also came to FAME in 1975, to record a couple of single releases that were issued on the Warner Brothers label. As we have seen, Charles Chalmers had already recorded at FAME, when he visited as one of the Chess artists sent down to Muscle Shoals to work with Rick Hall. The Rhodes sisters, Sandra and Donna, had also been before, along with Chalmers, to sing backing vocals on Candi Stanton's 1972 album "Candi Stanton". (Chalmers later married Sandra Rhodes).

The trio had started working together at Hi Records, where Willie Mitchell put them together to back Al Green on "Let's Stay Together" in 1971. They had subsequently built up an impressive list of clients, including Ann Peebles, Otis Clay, Mel & Tim, O.V. Wright, William Bell and many more. They recorded at Hi Records, Stax, FAME, Muscle Shoals Sound, Quad Studios in Nashville and at Malaco Studios, with some fantastic singers. Rick Hall hired them to work with Candi

Staton, Paul Anka, Z.Z. Hill, Mac Davis and Odia Coates. Incidentally, they also worked with Frank Sinatra. This list gives an indication of their versatility.

Now they had the opportunity to record under their own names at FAME. The two singles released in 1975 were "Out Of My Mind"/ "Would You Do It To Me Again" and "Look At Me and Love Me"/ "Just Someone You Had". The last-named song is a good example of their style. Donna Rhodes has a strong voice with a hint of Soul. The arrangements are by Jimmie Haskell. The song was written by FAME songwriters George Jackson and Raymond Moore. The production is smooth and romantic, a long way from the raw power of Aretha Franklin and Etta James.

*

White artists such as the Osmonds and Paul Anka were taking FAME Studios into new territory, moving away from Black R&B and finding new success on the Pop charts with White artists too. The musicians who made up the FAME Gang and the Muscle Shoals Horns were clearly capable and versatile. They were able to add to the appeal of FAME Studios for a wide range of artists, helping to create more hits and keeping Muscle Shoals in the industry spotlight.

Other artists who came to FAME to record were Bobbie Gentrie, Jerry Reed and the Gatlin Brothers. Through the eighties and nineties, the emphasis at FAME was on Country music, with major chart successes for T.G. Sheppard and the local group Shenandoah. In the new century, **Bettye LaVette** came to the studio in 2007 to record the album "The Scene of the Crime", backed Drive-By Truckers. It was co-produced by Patterson Hood, who is the son of David Hood. Both David (bass) and Spooner (Wurlitzer, grand piano) played on the session at FAME Studios. The last time they had previously played with Bettye LaVette was 35 years earlier at Muscle

Shoals Studios. Other musicians on the session were The Drive-By Truckers, Kelvin Holly (guitar), John Neff (Pedal steel guitar, guitar), Shonna Tucker (bass), Brad Morgan (drums), Mike Cooley (guitars), Patterson Hood (guitars) and the legendary Larry Byrom of Steppenwolf on guitar. The "Return To The Scene of The Crime" recording project was nominated for a Grammy Award in 2007 for "Best Contemporary Blues Album" (Vocal or Instrumental).

Recommended Track:

2007 Bettye LaVette: "I Still Want to Be Your Baby"

The **Nightowls** recorded their 2015 album "Fame Sessions" at the studio. Two of the old session men played on both these albums (David Hood and Spooner Oldham), which was very appropriate, as the band were trying to recapture the spirit of some of the early FAME output from Aretha Franklin and Wilson Pickett, albeit with a more modern spin.

There is a long list of visitors who were drawn to FAME to record, covering a wide range of genres. Gregg Allman (Blues), the Blind Boys of Alabama (Gospel), the Dixie Chicks (as they were called at that time), and many others, who all added to the legacy of Rick Hall's enterprise.

22

THE FAME STORY GOES ON

Rick Hall died in 2018, and his son Rodney took over. Rodney had started working at the studios in the early nineties, as a sound engineer and producer. He became general manager and then president, overseeing further developments at the studios.

A few months after the death of his father, Rodney met Glenn Rosenstein, a studio owner and record producer from Nashville. Rosenstein, a New Yorker who had worked at Sigma Sound, came to FAME to record a vocal track with one of his artists, and was struck by the quality of the sound. In an article on the Pro Sound website, he describes how special this studio is: "I flew the artist in from New York, put up a microphone and it was by far the best-sounding vocal room I'd heard in my life…" He suggested to Rodney that the control room in Studio B would benefit from an up-date. Rodney liked the idea, and they began to discuss what equipment to install. As luck would have it, Rosenstein found an SSL 6000 E mixing desk, that had come from a Dallas studio where Stevie Ray Vaughan had recorded several albums. The power supply and computer system were also upgraded. The console that had been built for Studio B in 1967 was brought back from a local museum and re-installed, alongside the SSL. During the renovations, they uncovered some of the wooden wall panelling that Rick Hall had used in 1961 and some of the original carpeting. The original tape storeroom was converted into an artist's lounge, with many of the old master tapes on display. The studio has been modernized, while retaining and even enhancing the magic of the original. The new studio was launched in 2019, along with a new website and the introduction of studio tours.

To celebrate the rebirth of FAME, Rodney Hall and producer

Keith Stegall brought together at FAME Studios a collection of current artists and session musicians, plus some of the old session men. The aim was to re-record some of the iconic songs from Muscle Shoals (combining FAME and Muscle Shoals Sound) as a tribute to those who had "built the brand". In keeping with the wide range of genres that Rick Hall had encouraged, the artists were chosen from a variety of musical backgrounds. The double album "Muscle Shoals – Small Town Big Sound" features sixteen excellent songs, sung by some well-known names. One stands out. Candi Staton, who sings "I Ain't Easy To Love" with Jason Isbell and John Paul White.

Rodney Hall is deeply aware of the special character of his father's creation:

"FAME Recording Studios brought out the best in so many incredibly talented musicians and performers. There was something about it — a magic, a mystique, an energy, a vibe — that drew music straight out of the souls of the performers. Its character has only seasoned with time." (FAME website)

The studio has been involved in recording or publishing records that have sold more than 350 million copies worldwide.

23

DEVELOPMENTS AT NORALA

Meanwhile, back at Norala Studio, Quin Ivy spent most of 1966 organising sessions for Percy Sledge. Jerry Wexler was happy for the tiny studio in the Shoals to keep on working with Atlantic's new R&B star. He knew from experience that it wasn't easy to create the sound that Percy Sledge had taken into the charts. He realised too that his company would benefit from all the attention that Quin Ivy and his team were going to give their number one performer. And that was more important than the fact that the studio only offered very basic technology.

Atlantic Records were planning to send a few of their existing Atco artists to Norala, in search of the Percy Sledge effect. They were also hoping that Quin Ivy would unearth more diamonds from the Muscle Shoals music mines. For this reason, they signed a new deal with Ivy in early 1967, promising to take material from any new artists that seemed to have the potential to break into the charts. Ivy set up a new record label, which he called South Camp, and the Norala label was abandoned.

June Edwards was the first singer singed to the new label. For the first single release, she recorded a Penn/Oldham song "My Man (My Sweet Man)" and a Spooner Oldham composition "Heaven Help Me (I'm Falling In Love With You)". Sadly, the single attracted little attention.

The next arrival at Norala was **Don Varner**, a young singer from Birmingham, Alabama. He recorded two songs in February 1967. The first was "Down In Texas", written by Eddie Hinton and Marlin Greene, followed by "Masquerade", another Eddie Hinton composition, co-written with Paul Ballenger. Once again, Atlantic were not tempted, despite some excellent guitar input from Marlin Greene, Junior Lowe and Hinton himself (on bass).

The first of the Atco artists arrived later in 1967. **Ted Taylor** was an experienced singer but needed a hit to convince Atlantic to keep him on their roster. He recorded a number of songs, two of which were selected for his next Atco single release: a Penn/ Oldham composition "Feed The Flame" and "Baby Come Back To Me". The A-side is a romantic Country ballad that Taylor infuses with Soul, with soaring vocal lines and falsetto frills. Quin Ivy must have been hopeful of a breakthrough, but the single failed to chart and Taylor moved on from Atlantic.

Percy Sledge returned to record his album "The Percy Sledge Way", featuring a series of covers. The band for the sessions included Spooner Oldham, Roger Hawkins and David Hood from FAME, plus Marlin Greene, Jerry Weaver and Eddie Hinton. The album and several singles charted, and Quin Ivy was happy.

He set about attracting new talent to the studio once more. **Tony Borders** came to Norala Studios in 1967 to record the first of a series of singles with Quin Ivy. Side A, "You Better Believe It", is a David Briggs/ Donny Fritts song, and side B is a song that Tony Borders had written called "What Kind of Spell". The single was released on the South Camp label.

Border returned to Norala later in the year to record six more songs, which Quin Ivy took successfully to Revue Records. "Cheaters Never Win", a Penn/ Oldham song, is backed by "Love and a Friend" by Billy Butler, released by Revue in 1968. The following year saw the release of another Penn/ Oldham song "I Met Her in Church", backed by "What Kind of Spell", recycled from South Camp, and then "Polly Wally", backed by "Gentle On My Mind".

In what was his most productive year, Tony Borders saw another of his Quin Ivy productions released on Uni Records. The "Lonely Weekend" single was backed by "You Better Believe".

In 1970 two more Border singles emerged on Quin Ivy's renamed own label. The first was "For My Woman's Love"/ "Please Don't Break My Heart", the second was "Promise To Myself"/ "Mix and Mingle".

While the earlier songs recorded by Borders at Norala were ballads, the later tracks were more up-tempo. The results were equally as good, which was no surprise. The session band consisted of Eddie Hinton and Junior Lowe (guitars), Roger Hawkins (drums), David Hood (bass) and a horn section made up of Gene "Bowlegs" Miller, James Mitchell and Aaron Varnell. As so often, the lack of publicity meant that the singles received little attention, far less than they deserved.

In 1988, the Japanese company True Sound Records issued a twelve-track compilation of Borders' songs. Better still, in 2007, the UK's Soulscape Records released a compilation album with eighteen tracks, making available several previously unreleased songs. They are well worth a listen.

Recommended Track:

1967 Tony Borders: "What Kind of Spell"

24

A CHANGE OF NAME FOR NORALA: NEW FACES AT QUINVY

In 1967 Quin Ivy decided to change the name of his studio and record label, to bring them into line with his publishing company. They all now became Quinvy.

Visitors included The Wee Juns, the Demon Brothers and Bill Brandon. The first two acts were seeking success in the Pop music field, but Brandon, a Black singer from Huntsville in Alabama, had a strong baritone voice that was suited to Soul and Gospel songs.

Bill Brandon recorded a number of excellent tracks at Quinvy, including "Self Preservation" (later recorded by Percy Sledge), "Full Grown Lovin' Man", "Since I Fell For You" and "Strangest Feeling". The first of these is a very good Country Soul ballad, produced by Spooner Oldham. The second is driving dance track. The third is a cover of an old Buddy Johnson song from 1948, and the last has a strong flavour of Blues, written by Penn and Oldham. The first two songs were issued Quin Ivy on his South Camp label in 1967. The last two were paired for release on a 1970 Quinvy single.

However, the best of Brandon's songs with Quin Ivy is "Rainbow Road", which Ivy leased to Tower Records in New York for 1968 release. It was written by Dan Penn and Donnie Fritts, probably with Arthur Alexander in mind, and Alexander did record the song later. Brandon's version fits the sad storyline perfectly, with horns and strings adding to the poignancy of the lyrics.

When these singles failed to gather any momentum, Brandon on, first to Moonsong Records in Birmingham, Alabama, and then to Prelude Records in New York. He recorded several singles and an album for Prelude at Wishbone Studios in the Shoals, and then left the music industry.

Recommended Track:

1968 Bill Brandon: "Rainbow Road"

Ben E. King came to Quinvy in May 1967 to record five tracks. Marlin Greene did all the arrangements and also produced the songs, along with Quin Ivy. The arrangements had been set up by Atco Records, who chose two of the songs for release on the label. The tracks in question were "Don't Take Your Sweet Love Away" and "She Knows What To Do For Me". The first was co-written by Marlin Greene and his wife Jeanie. The second was a Dr. John/ Jessie Hill song. Sadly, the single failed to make much impression.

Another significant 1967 arrival was **Eddie Hinton**. Born in Florida in 1944, Hinton had lived in Tuscaloosa, one of the Quad Cities since childhood. He was a White singer/songwriter and guitarist, who loved Black music and developed a style that was perfectly suited to Muscle Shoals R&B. Hinton was invited by Marlin Greene to play on sessions at Norala/ Quinvy from 1967. They wrote several songs together, including "Cover Me" and "It's All Wrong But It's Alright" for Percy Sledge. Hinton played on many of the recordings that Sledge undertook with Quin Ivy and his talents were well-known amongst the local session men.

Hinton went on to join sessions at FAME Studios and Muscle Shoals Sound Studios in addition to his work at Quinvy. His list of credits is impressive, including hits by Aretha Franklin, Arthur Conley, Wilson Pickett, the Staple Singers, and Johnny Taylor. Hinton played lead guitar on many well-known hits from Muscle Shoals.

He also recorded two albums in his own name during this period. The first was "Very Extremely Dangerous" released on the Capricorn Records label in 1978. The second, "Letters from Mississippi", was a compilation of six songs recorded with Jimmy Johnson in 1982 and some later tracks recorded at Birdland Recording Studio with John Wyker in 1986. Wyker called on Dan Penn, Spooner Oldham, and Donnie Fritts to help put the album together. This latter album was released in Europe and sparked interest in Hinton's work. His career was re-ignited, and a number of Soul-influenced Blues albums followed. Listen to the Hinton composition, "Hard Luck Guy", to see just how much Hinton owes to Otis Redding! The session band included Johnny Sandlin (drums), Spooner Oldham (Hammond B3 organ), Clayton Ivey (piano) and Eddie Hinton (guitar), with members of the Muscle Shoals Horns. Eddie Hinton died in 1995, at the age of 51.

Recommended Track:

1977 Eddie Hinton: "Hard Luck Guy"

In the first half of 1968, **James Carr** visited Quinvy, to record three songs, namely "Love Is a Beautiful Thing", "Life Turned Her That Way" and "That's the Way Love Turned Out for Me". He had also found time to record one track at FAME Studios in 1967, a George Jackson/ Raymond Moore song called "Search Your Heart".

After a long time in the vaults, the Quinvy tracks and the FAME song were released on an EP in 2011, entitled "In Muscle Shoals" by Kent Records in the UK and Goldwax in the USA. "Love Is a Beautiful Thing" is a classic, with beautiful horn arrangements and a lovely flute fill adding some real class.

Recommended Track: (recorded 1968)

2011 James Carr: "Love Is a Beautiful Thing"

Percy Sledge's continuing success enabled Quin Ivy to build a new studio in 1968. The new Quinvy Studio building was on Broadway in Sheffield, a little further out of town. The new studio had four-track recording equipment, which meant that overdubbing extra tracks now became possible. No longer did Ivy need to send tapes to Memphis or Miami to have strings or horns added. Other local recording venues had moved to eight or sixteen track machines, but four was enough for the improvements that Ivy wanted to make.

David Johnson was given the responsibility of managing the new studio by Quin Ivy. Johnson had worked at Norala with Ivy and now took on sound engineer duties. Johnson had met Ivy earlier, in fact. As a young teenager, Johnson used to go to the WLAY Radio station to speak with the DJs and listen to the music. Ivy gave him a job at his record store and later Johnson became a DJ at WLAY. When Ivy opened Norala Studios, Johnson turned up there too and was able to watch and learn. In 1969, the Swampers left FAME, which also meant that they were concentrating on their new venture at Muscle Shoals Sound Studios. As a result, they were no longer available for session work at Quinvy. Dan Penn and Spooner Oldham were together again at American Sound Studios in Memphis, and Marlin Greene, on whom Quin Ivy had depended since he opened

Norala, was finding work with the Swampers at MSS. It was a period of rapid change.Johnson took Greene's place as Ivy's right-hand man. New session musicians were brought in, including a number of the members of the FAME Gang, and the pattern set in 1967 and 1968 continued. Percy Sledge came to record new material when he could fit sessions in between his live performances. Other less well-known artists came in search of elusive success. In 1969, Quin Ivy sold the old Norala premises to James Thomas and Billy Cofield, the sax player who had played on Percy Sledge's original version of "When A Man Loves A Woman" alongside Don Pollard.

Z.Z. HILL IN MUSCLE SHOALS

Arzell Hill was born in Naples, Texas, in 1935. He was a member of the Spiritual Five Gospel group in his twenties, and then began performing as a solo artist, inspired by Sam Cooke and Bobby Bland. He wrote some of the songs for his shows and was drawn to Soul and Blues. His stage name was chosen in imitation of B.B. King.

In 1963 Hill went to Los Angeles to work with his brother Matt Hill, who was starting out as a record producer. His first single "You Were Wrong" drew the attention of Kent Records (not the UK label), who offered Hill a contract. He didn't stay with Kent very long, and by 1969 he had signed up with Quin Ivy in the Shoals.

The first session in May was supervised by Bob Wilson, who came over from Nashville. The Swampers had just left FAME to set up their own studio and were therefore not available, so new musicians were brought in: Tim Drummond, Butch Owens, Jimmy Evans and Don Walker were joined by Wilson on keyboards. Two tracks were completed: "(Home Just Ain't Home At) Suppertime" and "It's a Hang Up Baby". The plan was to interest Atlantic Records, in the hope that they would lease the tracks, just as had happened for Percy Sledge. The Atlantic single was duly released, but there was very little support for the songs from Atlantic and they soon lost interest.

Hill returned to the studio in October to record seven more tracks in three days, two of which were "Faithful and True" (written by Marlin and Jeanie Green and Dan Penn) and "I Think I'd Do It", which were chosen for the next single. The band assembled for the sessions included Butch Owens, Jimmy Evans, Jasper Guarino and Ronnie Oldham, a local Florence keyboard player. When Atlantic failed to pick up any of the tracks for a second single, Quin Ivy decided to release the single on his own Quinvy label. Hill was not impressed! He returned to Los Angeles to work with his brother again, and Quin Ivy sold the contract to Jerry Williams, along with rights to the Z.Z. Hill songs already in the can.

Strangely, in 1971, Hill was persuaded by new producer Jerry "Swamp Dogg" Williams to return to Quinvy Studios. He agreed, as long as Quin Ivy stayed away! Williams assembled a session band that included most of the musicians used for the earlier sessions, plus Bob Wray, Jesse Carr and Fred Proudy. Williams also brought in Chuck Leavell, Charles Hayward and Lou Mullenix. Clayton Ivey and Swamp Dogg shared keyboard duties with Ronnie Oldham. James Mitchell and Gene "Bowlegs" Miller were added to the horn section. It was a strong line-up. Some of the earlier songs were probably re-worked and several new tracks were added. When the final session was finished, Williams released Hill from his contract, in exchange for full payment of all outstanding royalties.

The resulting album, entitled "The Brand New Z.Z. Hill", was released in 1971, charting at number one hundred and ninety-four on the Billboard 200 album chart. Several singles taken from the album also made chart entries, but only in the lower echelons. "Faithful and True" reached the top one hundred and "Chokin' Kind" went to number fifty. "It Ain't No Use" was the most successful, reaching number thirty-four on the R&B chart in 1972. That doesn't sound too impressive, but the album has a number of very good songs.

The album is unusual in that side one is set out as a three-act Blues opera, with spoken introductions. Side two is formatted normally, with five songs. Track 1 "It Ain't No Use" is a straight Blues number. Track 2 "Ha Ha (The Laughing Song)" is funkier, with some nice horn sections. Track 3, "Second Chance", is a smooth Soul song, that shows off Hill's voice to good effect. Track 4 is an up-tempo dance track, followed by "Faithful and True", which concludes the opera. It is a slow ballad with Hill singing in Otis Redding style, featuring a strong organ line.

Side two dispenses with the spoken sections and is better for that. The songs are all Soul tracks, with "A Man Needs a Woman – Woman Needs a Man" nodding in the direction of Nashville Country. There is considerable variation in the style and arrangements of the songs, and Z.Z. Hill takes everything in his stride.

Hill went back to work with his brother once more and linked up with United Artists. In 1974, he returned to the Shoals area, not to Quinvy this time but to FAME Studios, where he recorded the "Z.Z." album for United Artists, with his brother Matt directing operations. Some of the FAME Gang were called on for the recording sessions, including Roger Clark (drums), Ken Bell (guitar), Tim Henson (keyboards), and the Muscle Shoals Horns. Rhodes, Chalmers, Rhodes sang backing vocals.

Two songs from the album entered the R&B charts, "Let Them Talk" and Hill's own composition "Am I Grooving You". As on Hill's Quinvy album, there is a range of styles, from romantic ballads ("Let Them Talk" and "You're Killing Me") to Blues ("Bad Mouth and Gossip"). "Am I Groovin' You" and "Clean Up America" are funky. The songs on the B-side of the album are typical Muscle Shoals Country Soul. The songs are drawn from a range of sources, with only "It Ain't Safe" written by the FAME songwriters Clarence Carter and George Jackson. Some of the songs are a little too repetitive and the whole album would surely have benefitted from some input from Rick Hall.

When his brother Matt suddenly died, Hill moved to Columbia Records. In 1979, he switched to Malaco Records and had success with some fine songs, including two George Jackson compositions, "Cheating in the Next Room" and "Down Home Blues".

Z.Z. Hill died in 1984, two months after being involved in a serious car accident.

The songs that Hill recorded in the Shoals have been issued on various compilation albums, starting in 1984. Jerry "Swamp Dogg" Williams took seven of the Quinvy album masters to Los Angeles and re-mixed them, with new backing musicians, with resulting new versions appearing on an album entitled "Thrill On The (Z.Z.) Hill" on the Rare Bullet label. Ace Records in the UK issued a two-album CD in 1994, pairing Hill's album with Freddie North's "Friend" album.

Then in 1996, Capitol Records issued a collection of all Hill's United Artists recordings from 1972 to 1975, which includes the tracks recorded at FAME, with the title "The Complete Hill Records Collection".

In 2002, Jerry Williams himself re-issued the original Hill album, with the addition of eleven bonus tracks. For the first time, all the Quinvy recordings were available on one CD, along with six of the Los Angeles reworked songs (only the new version of "Touch 'Em With Love" is missing).

Recommended Tracks:

1971 Z.Z. Hill: "Faithful and True" (recorded 1969)

1974 Z.Z. Hill: "It Ain't Safe"

1974 Z.Z. Hill: "Am I Groovin' You"

26

QUINVY BECOMES BROADWAY

Visitors to Quinvy in 1970 included Tony Borders, Buddy Causey and Lynyrd Skynyrd, who came to cut a few demos but also to offer their services as session men. Quin Ivy was not impressed! It didn't take long for the band to move across to Muscle Shoals Sound Studios to start working with Jimmy Johnson. During that year, further up-grades were made to the recording equipment, bringing an eight-track facility to Quinvy.

By 1971 Quin Ivy was spending more time looking after his other business interests, leaving David Johnson to run the studio on more occasions. Jerry Williams (otherwise known as Swamp Dogg), who had brought Z.Z. Hill back to Quinvy in 1971, soon brought more artists from his Mankind Records roster, helping to boost the studio's income at a time when Percy Sledge's success was beginning to tail off.

Doris Duke's Kent Soul album

(used with permission of Ace Records UK)

Doris Duke had teamed up with producer Williams in 1969 to record an excellent album, "I'm a Loser", at Capricorn Sound Studio, which was released on Canyon Records in 1970. In 1971 they came to Quinvy to record tracks for Duke's second album, "A Legend in Her Own Time", with a session band that included Jasper Guarino (drums), Jesse Carr (guitar), Chuck Leavell and Williams on keyboards, with strings added by the Philadelphia Symphony Orchestra at Regent Sound Studios. Backing vocalists were Charles Chalmers, Sandra Rhodes and Jeanie Greene (Marlin Greene's wife). The album was released in 1971 on Mankind Records in the USA and on Mojo Records in the UK. In 2013 Ace Records re-issued the album on its Kent Soul imprint.

Recommended Tracks:

1971 Doris Duke: "Since I Fell For You"

Brooks O'Dell was next to arrive. He was already an experienced performer who had recorded for several labels before signing for Mankind and coming to Quinvy with Williams. He recorded eleven tracks, with two singles being released in 1971 and 1972. The remaining tracks didn't see the light of day until the album "I'm Your Man" was released on the UK label Kent Records in 2008.

Brooks O'Dell's album "I'm Your Man" on Kent Records
(used with permission of Ace Records UK)

The third of the Mankind artists to visit Quinvy in 1971 was **Freddie North**. He was an experienced singer from Nashville, who had been recording for a variety of small labels without success since 1959. Jerry Williams set out to put that right. North's first single recorded in the Shoals was "She's All I Got", written by Williams and Gary Bonds. The song entered the charts, reaching number ten on the R&B chart and number thirty-nine on the Pop chart. On the strength of this success, North completed his second album "Friend", from which another single was released entitled "You and Me Together Forever". This song also entered the R&B chart, reaching number twenty -six.

North's single successes helped promote the album, which spent four weeks on the Billboard R&B Album Chart at the start of 1972. When subsequent singles failed to chart, North ended the arrangement with Williams and concentrated on his business interests. Surprisingly, he returned to the Shoals in 1977 to record another album with David Johnson at the renamed Broadway Sound Studio, which was re-issued in 1989 on UK Charly Records with a new title "I'm Your Man". These two albums contain some excellent Country Soul songs, including "I'm Your Man" and "If This is the Last Time".

In 1994, the UK's Ace Records released a two-album CD combining North's "Friend" album with Z.Z. Hill's "The Brand New Z.Z. Hill", with the title "Swamp Dogg Presents The Brand New Z.Z. Hill/Friend".

Later visitors included Ernie Shelby, Marlin Greene and Bette Williams. When Quin Ivy decided that he wanted to move away from the music business in 1973, he sold the studio to David Johnson. It was soon renamed and relaunched as Broadway Sound, later to welcome Freddie North, James Govan, Sandra Wright and many others.

Quin Ivy went off to study, gaining a degree in accountancy. In 1980 he started teaching at the University of North Alabama and remained there until his retirement in 1996.

Johnson ran Broadway Sound until 1989, when he was appointed Executive Director of the Alabama Music Hall of Fame, a position he held for over twenty years.

Recommended Tracks:

1971 Freddie North: "Raining on a Sunny Day"

1971 Freddie North: "Cuss the Wind"

27

THE SWAMPERS BUILD A NEW STUDIO

When the Swampers left FAME in 1969, they moved into a building at 3614 Jackson Highway. It was an old warehouse in Sheffield, where coffins had been stored, opposite a cemetery. In 1967 Jimmy Johnson had helped the owner, Fred Bevis, turn it into a four-track recording studio. Some of the local musicians and songwriters had rented space there to work, but things didn't as well as Bevis had hoped, so he decided to sell the property. He offered it to Roger Hawkins, who persuaded the others that it was an opportunity not to be missed. Any doubts were settled when Jerry Wexler offered financial and artist support, and the sale was agreed. The four session men were co-owners, the first to own their own studio.

Their first task was to upgrade the equipment to an eight-track system. They were then ready to go. Wexler provided the first client, the Pop singer **Cher**, who came to Muscle Shoals Sound to record her sixth album, marking the opening of the new facility by naming her album "3614 Jackson Highway". Boz Scaggs then arrived to record his 1969 album "Boz Scaggs", with Duane Allman playing lead guitar on several tracks.

Just like Rick Hall at FAME, the Swampers took the decision to invite artists from all genres to their studio, but there were still opportunities to produce excellent R&B music. It was indeed an R&B song that achieved the first big hit for the new studio, when in August 1969 **R.B. Greaves**, another Atlantic artist, came to record a song that he had written, called "Take a Letter Maria".

3614, Jackson Highway

Photo: Dailynetworks 2007 (Wikimedia Commons)

Greaves was a nephew of Sam Cooke, with a similar smooth, rich voice. The single sold well, rising to number two on the Billboard Hot 100, selling over two million copies by 1970, achieving gold certification. It was the first hit for the Swampers, who were joined for the session by Eddie Hinton (guitar), Mel Lastie (trumpet) and Donna Jean Thatcher (later Godchaux), who sang the backing vocal. Producers were Ahmet Ertegun of Atlantic Records and Marlin Greene, who had switched from Norala Studio to Muscle Shoals Sound.

Recommended Track:

1969 R.B. Greaves: "Take a Letter, Maria"

Just a few weeks later, the UK female solo artist **Lulu** recorded a now-classic album in Muscle Shoals which was not a major hit record but had some outstanding tracks, according to many music historians and music industry critics. The album "New Routes" was recorded between September

10th and October 2nd 1969 at Muscle Shoals Sound Studio. It was one of that facility's earliest recordings, the album being released on January 16th 1970 in America. The album was the debut release for Lulu on the Atco Records label, a music division of Atlantic Records, co-produced by the legendary Atlantic Records team of Tom Dowd, Arif Mardin and Jerry Wexler.

Only one single was released from the album, called "Oh Me Oh My (I'm a Fool for You Baby)", which gradually accrued enough popularity to reach the Top 30 of the Billboard Hot 100 in February 1970. During the same month, "New Routes" debuted on the Billboard 200 Albums Chart on its way to number eighty-eight. The album produced no further A-sides, but in May 1970 the track "Where's Eddie" was utilised to back "Hum a Song (From Your Heart)", the advance single from her next studio album "Melody Fair".

Many performances by Lulu on United States television channels helped to break the single "Oh Me Oh My..." into the Billboard Hot 100 Singles Chart in December 1969 and then buoy the track, as it gradually gained momentum to become Lulu's first Top 30 hit since "To Sir With Love", at the end of February 1970. "Oh Me Oh My..." would peak at number twenty-two in March 1970 on the Cash Box Pop Singles chart listing.

Recommended Track:

1969 Lulu: "Sweep Around Your Own Back Door"

Lulu was followed in December by some surprising visitors from the UK. **The Rolling Stones** arrived at Muscle Shoals on December 2nd in 1969 for a short recording session to see if they could, assisted by Jimmy Johnson the chief sound engineer at the studio, create a sound that had a Rolling

Stones feel mixed with a Muscle Shoals signature sound. Keith Richards has remarked on the effect it had on them: "I thought it was one of the easiest and rockin'est sessions that we'd ever done. I don't think we've been quite so prolific ever. I mean, we cut three or four tracks in two days."

The results were dynamic and powerful, with the lead single "Brown Sugar" going to number one on the Billboard Hot 100 Singles Chart week-ending May 29th 1971 (2 weeks). Contractual issues delayed the release of the album that the Rolling Stones were making. The tracks recorded at Muscle Shoals were eventually included on the album "Sticky Fingers" which peaked at number one on the Billboard Top 200 Albums Chart in May 1971 (4 weeks). The album also did extremely in the UK by reaching the number one position on the UK Official Pop Albums Chart week-ending May 8th 1971 (5 weeks).

The single "Brown Sugar" sold in excess of a quarter of a million copies in the UK and was awarded a silver disc by the BPI on November 1st 1975. The "Sticky Fingers" album did very well in France and was awarded gold certification for selling over one hundred thousand copies in that country and peaked at number three on the French SNEP Albums Chart. The album was number one in nine different music markets across the world. In the United States at present the album has eventually achieved triple-platinum status for over three million copies sold, according to the RIAA.

The single "Brown Sugar" also received gold certification in America for over one million copies sold according to the RIAA. The other Muscle Shoals songs were "Wild Horses" and "You Gotta Move". The last of these was recorded first on the first night of their two-day session. It is a traditional Gospel song, recorded in 1965 by Mississippi Fred McDowell. Mick Jagger chose the song to celebrate being in Alabama!

Recommended Tracks:

1971 The Rolling Stones: "Brown Sugar" (recorded 1969)

1971 The Rolling Stones: "You Gotta Move" (1969)

The Swampers now had two gold discs and a number one. Unfortunately, Jerry Wexler had had second thoughts about using Muscle Shoals and switched his artists to a studio in Florida. The threat to the new studio was obvious, but the word spread that the boys from FAME were open for business. Next to come were Mel & Tim, followed by the Staple Singers. **Mel & Tim** had had one hit in Chicago, before Barry Beckett brought them to Muscle Shoals to record "Starting All Over Again". Stax Records in Memphis picked the recording up and released it in 1972. The single spent five months on the charts in the USA, reaching number four on the R&B chart and number nineteen on the Pop chart.

Recommended Track:

1972 Mel & Tim: "Starting All Over Again"

The Staple Singers were well-known when they came to Muscle Shoals Sound Studios in 1971. Having started their recording career in Chicago, they had teamed up with Steve Cropper at Stax in Memphis to consolidate their breakthrough into the mainstream of secular music.

In 1970 things changed. Steve Cropper left Stax and Pervis left the group. Sister Yvonne took over from Pervis, and Al Bell replaced Steve Cropper as producer. Bell's first decision was to switch the centre of operations to Muscle Shoals. He brought the Staple Singers to Muscle Shoals Sound Studios to work with the famous Rhythm Section, known as the Swampers.

The first album master-minded by Bell was "The Staple Swingers", released in 1971, which entered the Soul Albums chart, reaching number nine. Three singles were taken from the album, "Love Is Plentiful", "Heavy Makes You Happy (Sha-Na-Boom Boom)" and "You've Got to Earn It", which all charted on the R&B Singles chart. Their popularity was growing! The songs on the album were written by a wide variety of songwriters, including several of the Stax in-house team, plus Maurice and Barry Gibb of the Bee Gees and Pops Staples too. Strings and horns were provided by the Memphis Symphony Orchestra and the Muscle Shoals Horns, with the Bar-Kays responsible for some of the horn arrangements. Final production work was carried out by Bell and Terry Manning at Ardent Studios in Memphis. There was a lot of Stax input, but the Swampers drove the songs, and that, of course, is why Al Bell brought them to Muscle Shoals rather than record the album in Memphis.

The follow-up album, "Be Altitude: Respect Yourself", finally sealed their break-through, reaching number three on the R&B Albums chart and number nineteen on the Pop chart. Again, three singles from the album broke into the national charts: "Respect Yourself" (number nine Pop and number two R&B), "I'll Take You There" (number one on both charts) and "This World" (thirty-eight Pop and six R&B). The style is now much funkier, with a dance beat. "I'll Take You There" adds some reggae too, with the inspiration coming from Al Bell, who wrote the song.

Musicians involved in the session were Jimmy Johnson, Raymond Banks, and Eddie Hinton (guitars), Barry Beckett (Wurlitzer electronic piano), Roger Hawkins (drums), and David Hood (bass), plus Ben Cauley from the Bar-Kays (trumpet), and the South Memphis horns. Horn and string arrangements were done by Johnny Allen and recorded at Artie Fields recording studio in Detroit. The finishing touches were added in Memphis at Ardent Studios by Terry Manning, who overdubbed guitar, Moog synthesizer, mellotron and harmonica parts. Al Bell oversaw production. With the help of the Swampers, the songs from this album have become classics in the field of Gospel-tinged Soul.

The Staple Singers in 1974 with Don Cornelius

Publicity Photo for Soul Train (Wikimedia Commons)

There were two further albums on Stax, "Be What You Are" (1973) and "City in the Sky" (1974), which both charted to number thirteen on the R&B Albums chart. Four singles reached the top four of the R&B Singles chart, with the most successful "If You're Ready (Come Go with Me)" spending three weeks at number one on the Hot Soul Singles chart in 1973. Everything looked set fair, but in 1975 Stax ran into financial difficulties and the family moved back to Chicago.

Recommended Track:

1971 The Staple Singers: "You've Got To Earn It"

1972 The Staple Singers: "I'll Take You There"

Around the same time as the Staple Singers were putting these songs together, a new American rock band came to work at the studios, with the unusual name of **Lynyrd Skynyrd**. The recorded a number of songs for their first album, before the decision was taken to shelve those tracks when they failed to attract a record company to release them. They started again elsewhere and did well. When several members of the band were killed in a plane crash in 1977, it was decided to release the early material as a posthumous compilation album with the album given the ironic title "Skynyrd's First and … Last". The album was re-released in 1998, with eight additional tracks, with a new name "Skynyrd's First: The Complete Muscle Shoals Album".

It was this band that gave the four session men who owned the studio an additional push towards iconic status by writing about them in one of their songs, "Sweet Home Alabama":

Now Muscle Shoals has got The Swampers
And they've been known to pick a song or two (yes they do)
Lord they get me off so much
They pick me up when I'm feeling blue, now how 'bout you?

28

BOBBY WOMACK IN MUSCLE SHOALS

Bobby Womack's career started in the mid-fifties, when he started touring with his family group the Valentinos, mentored by Sam Cooke. He had taught himself to play guitar, using the standard right-handed tuning, even though Womack was left-handed and turned the guitar over to play it. It didn't seem to present much of a problem for him, as he went on to become Sam Cooke's backing guitarist.

Around 1965 Womack started recording as a solo artist, for a number of labels including Checker in Chicago, owned by Chess Records, before he moved to Memphis. There he worked at Chips Moman's American Sound Studio as a session guitarist and songwriter. He signed for Minit Records in New Orleans in 1968, recording three albums, and then switched to United Artists. It was now that Womack came to Muscle Shoals Sound Studios to record with the Swampers.

Bobby Womack's debut album on United Artist Records was recorded at the Muscle Shoals Sound Studio with instrumental support from key members of the Muscle Shoals Rhythm Section. The album, entitled "Communication", did extremely well on the Billboard Hot Soul Albums chart by reaching number five. It was originally recorded in 1971. This was his first solo album to reach the Top 10 of the Billboard Hot Soul Albums Chart. The classic R&B and Soul single released from the album was "That's The Way I Feel About Cha" which became a number two on the Billboard Hot Soul Singles Chart in 1972, selling in excess of eight hundred thousand copies in the United States. The track features the guitar riff of Jimmy Johnson, of course, one of the key musicians and chief engineer at Muscle Shoals Sound Studio, where the entire album was recorded.

This started a four-year creative output of albums and singles that were mainly recorded at Muscle Shoals Sound Studio. The next album, entitled "Understanding", was recorded partly at Muscle Shoals Sound Studio and partly at American Sound Studio in Memphis (made famous for recording Elvis Presley's comeback album "From Elvis in Memphis" that became gold-certified). The first single released from "Understanding" was "Woman's Gotta Have It". The song reached number one on the Billboard Hot Soul Singles Chart week-ending June 17th 1972 (1 week). This was Womack's first song, co-written with Linda Cooke Womack (daughter of the late Sam Cooke) and Darryl Cater, to go to the top position on a Billboard singles chart since he started recording as a solo artist in the 1960s.

The hit single was recorded at American Sound Studio; personnel on the track included Mike Leech on bass, Reggie Young on guitar, Hayward Bishop on drums and percussion, Bobby Wood on piano and Bobby Emmons on organ and Mike Leech also did the string arrangements. He actually began laying down the track at Muscle Shoals Sound Studio before finally completing the recording in Memphis. Four tracks were recorded in Memphis. The remaining six tracks on the album were recorded at Muscle Shoals Sound Studio. The B side of the single "Woman's Gotta Have It" called "Harry Hippie" became a favourite for black DJs across America, which helped the single sell in excess of one million copies, bringing a gold disc from the RIAA on February 14th 1973. It peaked at number eight on the same singles chart listing as the number one single from the album.

The following album "Facts of Life" produced another major hit for Womack, with the single "Nobody Wants You When You're Down and Out". The song peaked at number two on the Billboard Hot Soul Singles Chart in 1973. The album also charted at number six on the Billboard Hot Soul Albums Chart that same year. Womack obtained another one million-seller with "Lookin' for a Love", gold-certified on April 8th 1974. The song was extracted from the parent album "Lookin' for a Love

Again" which reached number five on the Billboard Hot Soul Albums Chart that year and became Womack's best performance so far while he was collaborating with the Muscle Shoals Rhythm Section over a four-year period during the early to mid-1970s.

The importance of the songs that Womack recorded at Muscle Shoals Sound Studios was recognised in 1992 in France, with the release of a compilation album of seventeen tracks entitled "In Muscle Shoals" on the Editions Atlas label.

A similar compilation, with fifteen tracks, appeared in 1998 on Legacy/ Columbia. The album contains two duets. The first is "Trust Your Heart" with David Ruffin, and the second is "Stop Before We Start", with Candi Staton.

Recommended Track:

1971 Bobby Womack: "That's The Way I Feel About Cha"

Bobby Womack

Photo: Bill Ebbesen: 2010 (Wikimedia Commons)

29

THE SWAMPERS' FAME SPREADS

During the next seven years, the studio attracted some big names from the Pop music world and established itself alongside FAME Studios as a centre of excellence. **Paul Simon** came in 1973, looking for the reggae sound that he had heard on the Staple Singers' hits from Muscle Shoals, and was surprised to find an all-white rhythm section. He was even more surprised when he gave the Swampers details of his song "Kodachrome" and had the finished article in the can after just two takes. The Muscle Shoals Rhythm Section, to give the Swampers their more formal name, were talented, versatile, and very quick!

Simon recorded a second song "Loves Me Like a Rock" and went away happy. Both tracks were released as singles, and both reached number two on the Billboard Pop chart. The second single, "Loves Me Like A Rock", achieved number one on two occasions in 1973, on different singles chart listings in America. It went to number one on the Billboard Adult Contemporary Singles Chart week-ending September 8th (2 weeks) and also to number one on the Cashbox Magazine Pop Singles Chart week-ending September 29th. Both songs feature on the album "There Goes Rhymin' Simon".

The English rock band **Traffic** recorded an album entitled "Shoot Out at the Fantasy Factory" at Muscle Shoals Sound Studio in the early 1970s, which achieved gold certification on March 3rd 1973 according to the RIAA. The album features several members of Muscle Shoals Rhythm Section playing on several different instruments on the project, with Barry Beckett on keyboards on the track "Tragic Magic" and Jimmy Johnson playing clarinet on the same track. David Hood, guitar, and Roger Hawkins, drums, are featured on the majority of the tracks on the album.

The Stax artist **Johnnie Taylor** recorded parts of several albums with the Muscle Shoals Rhythm Section, between 1970 and 1977. The first Stax album to feature the Muscle Shoals Rhythm section was "One Step Beyond" in 1970, with Larry Hamby as sound engineer. Four tracks were recorded at Muscle Shoals Sound Studio out of the eight tracks on the album. These tracks were "Time After Time", "I Am Somebody (Parts I & II)", "I Don't Wanna Lose You (Parts I & II)" and "Don't Take My Sunshine".

This was followed by the 1973 release "Taylored In Silk" studio album, with most of the tracks recorded at Muscle Shoals Sound Studio, except "Talk To Me", which was recorded at United Sounds Studios, Detroit, Michigan. The string parts were recorded at A & R Recording in New York, with final mixing done in Detroit. The first track on the album is "We Are Careless With Our Love". It is in my view a sweet Southern Soul performance by the rhythm section with beautiful strings and horns accompaniment, arranged by former Motown string and horn arranger Wade Marcus.

Another interesting deep Southern Soul treatment by producer Don Davis (with sound engineering support from Jerry Master) is evident on "Standing In For Jody", which was not included on the original recording, but later added as a bonus track. Master was able to capture the vibe in the studio with the rhythm section on great form.

The organ part played (presumably) by Barry Beckett on "Starting All Over Again" is out of this world. He also did a brilliant job on "Cheaper To Keep Her", performing a solo piece throughout the track behind Johnnie Taylor's voice, with the other rhythm section members in the background. The recording of the Blues composition "I am Doing My Own Thing Part 1" (another later addition) shows the versatility of the rhythm section. Johnnie Taylor was in in his element and sounds like a worshipper with the dynamic female vocalists in support. Key elements of the sound come from the brilliant keyboard performance of Barry Beckett and Jimmy Johnson's guitar workout, driving an explosive groove.

The track "I Believe In You (You Believe In Me)" became a number one single on the Billboard Hot Soul Singles Chart week-ending 21st July 1973 (2 weeks). The entire Muscle Shoal Rhythm section played on the song. The song became Johnnie Taylor's last gold single for Stax Records.

The following track on the album, "One Thing Is Wrong With My Woman", is a beautiful track full of drama. It is a powerful love story, expressed with rich Southern emotion. Johnnie Taylor sings with great vocal control and authority.

The last two tracks on the album, "I Can Read Between The Lines" and "This Bitter Earth", show again the perfect balance achieved by the sound engineers in Detroit, with the strings and horns recorded at United Sound System Studios in Detroit and the rhythm laid down at Muscle Shoals Sound Studio combining beautifully.

Taylor switched to Columbia Records, when Stax went out of business in 1975. His first album for the new label was a major hit. "Eargasm" was certified gold on 5th April 1976 and eventually went platinum on 7th November 2001. All four key members of the Muscle Shoal rhythm section contributed to the album, with David Hood on bass, Roger Hawkins on drums, with Jimmy Johnson on rhythm guitar and Barry Beckett on keyboards.

Two tracks, "Please Don't Stop (That Song From Playing)" and "Running Out of Lies", demonstrate the Southern Soul and R&B funky groove of Muscle Shoals, with David Hood's bassline patterns counter-balanced by Roger Hawkins' pulsating drum beats, hard and soft as the song moves along. "Pick Up The Pieces", with a groovy bottom line accompanied by dynamic horns and strings, has a timeless quality that certainly separates it and the other Muscle Shoals tracks from "Disco Lady", which was recorded at United Sound Systems in Detroit. The rhythm section that played on the hit track also played regularly with George Clinton on his Parliament, Bootsy's Rubber Band and Funkadelic recordings. The contrast is very clear.

The follow-up studio album "Rated Extraordinary", released in 1977, also featured the Muscle Shoal rhythm section on several tracks, with backing vocals from Brandy (the backing vocalists for Millie Jackson). Some of the tracks on the studio album were also recorded at United Sound System Studios in Detroit.

It is obvious from listening to these Johnnie Taylor albums that the drummer and bass player are the fundamental anchor to any recording, as it develops in the recording studio. The pulsating signature sound drumbeats of the late Roger Hawkins, paired with David Hood's raw, refined, and complex rhythm patterns on bass, is the heartbeat of the signature sound of Muscle Shoals.

Recommended Track:

1973 Johnnie Taylor: "I Believe In You (You Believe In Me)"

Rod Stewart also came to Muscle Shoals, first in 1974/5 and again in 1976, and experienced great success, with two albums in succession becoming best-sellers with the help of the Muscle Shoals Rhythm Section and with the legendary Atlantic Records sound engineer Tom Dowd in charge of production. The session men at Muscle Shoals Studios were some of star performers who collaborated with Rod Stewart on the album "Atlantic Crossing", which was gold-certified in America after it was released on August 15th 1975. Several members of The Memphis Horns and Booker T & The MGs added their creative touch to the overall sound of the album, helping it go to number one on the UK Official Pop Albums Chart on two occasions, starting week-ending August 30th 1975 (4 weeks) and again on October 11th 1975 (1 week). During the same period in 1975, the album received platinum certification in the UK from the BPI for over three hundred thousand copies sold and also gold certification from the RIAA in America for over half a million copies sold.

The follow-up album "A Night On The Town" was another success for Stewart, out-selling the previous release by an extra half a million copies in the United States, going to platinum status with over one million copies sold according to the RIAA. The album became another number one for Rod Stewart on the UK Official Pop Albums Chart week-ending July 10th 1976 (1 week). The album was also number one in four other countries around the world. It went on to achieve multi-platinum status in America for over two million copies sold according to the RIAA and was also awarded platinum certification in the UK by the BPI for over three hundred thousand copies sold.

No doubt inspired by the success of Paul's Simon's brief visit to Muscle Shoals, **Art Garfunkel** recorded one of the songs for his album "Breakaway" with the session men from Muscle Shoals, David Hood, Roger Hawkins, Barry Beckett, and Pete Carr on guitar. The track in question is "My Little Town", a Paul Simon song, notable for bringing the duo back together in 1975 after five years working as solo artists.

During the same year **Bob Seger** made the first of many visits to the Swampers' studio. Seger had a succession of platinum and multi-platinum albums entirely and partially recorded at Muscle Shoals Studio. His first certified multi-platinum album (two million copies sold) was entitled "Beautiful Loser", released by Capitol Records on the April 12th 1975. Most of the album was recorded with the session musicians from the Muscle Shoals Rhythm Section. The producers on the album were Barry Beckett, Roger Hawkins, David Hood,

Jimmy Johnson, Spooner Oldham, and Bob Seger himself. The album features the powerful presence of the Muscle Shoals Horn Section on several tracks.

His next studio album was a bigger success in terms of sales, going five times platinum in America alone. The album "Night Moves" was Bob Seger's ninth studio album and his first with the Silver Bullet Band. It was released in October 1976. Although the front cover only credits backing by the Silver Bullet Band, four of the nine songs on the album feature backing by the Muscle Shoals Rhythm Section, who also shared production duties with Punch Andrews (Bob Seger's manager), Bob Seger and Jack Richardson. Seger's next album with the Silver Bullet Band was just as successful as "Night Moves".

The album "Stranger in Town", released by Capitol Records on May 5th 1978, became an instant success in America by achieving platinum certification within a month of its release. "Stranger in Town" also did very well in the UK by obtaining gold certification from the BPI for over one hundred thousand copies sold. This was Seger's first studio album with the group to achieve such a status in England. The album went on to sell in large numbers in America just like its predecessor, reaching six-times platinum certification according to the RIAA. The Silver Bullet Band, just as on the previous album, backed Seger on about half of the songs and the Muscle Shoals Rhythm Section backed Seger on the other half.

The eleventh studio album by American rock singer Bob Seger and his third with The Silver Bullet Band was called "Against the Wind". The album was released in 1980. It is Seger's only number one album on the Billboard 200 Albums Chart, reaching that position week-ending May 3rd 1980 (six weeks) and knocking Pink Floyd's massive-selling "The Wall" from the top position. The album also earned two Grammy Awards in 1981 for "Best Recording Package" and "Best Rock Performance By A Duo Or Group with Vocal". It was also a best-seller for Seger, his third to achieve multi-platinum status with over five million copies sold in the United States according to the RIAA.

Bob Seger and the Silver Bullet Band achieved platinum status once again with their late 1982 album "The Distance", which came out in December of that year. It didn't manage to repeat the success of its predecessor by going to number one but managed to achieve great success on the Billboard Adult Contemporary Singles Chart with the song "Shame on the Moon", which went to number one week-ending February 12th 1983 (2 weeks). The song was at number two for four weeks from week-ending February 26th 1983 and was kept from the top position on the Billboard Hot 100 Singles Chart by "Baby, Come To Me" performed by Patti Austin & James Ingram for the first two weeks and for the remaining two weeks by "Billie Jean" performed by the late Michael Jackson.

The final Seger album that features any member of the Muscle Shoals Rhythm Section was the studio album "The Fire Inside", for which Barry Beckett produced four tracks. The album was certified platinum in both Canada and America during 1991. All previous studio-released albums from 1976 with Bob Seger and the group were either platinum or multi-platinum certifications in Canada. In recognition of Bob Seger's tremendous success over five decades, he was inducted into the Rock and Roll Hall of Fame in 2004 and the Songwriters Hall of Fame in 2012.

The Muscle Shoals Studio band had further success with another UK Pop artist by the name of **Cat Stevens** (before he converted to Islam and adopted the name Yusuf Islam). The studio album they worked on was entitled "Izitso". It was released on May 28th 1977 on A&M Records. The Muscle Shoals Rhythm Section only played on two tracks on the album, "Killin' Time" and "Child for a Day". On the session were David Hood on double bass, bass and bass synthesizer, Barry Beckett on piano, electric piano, organ and keyboards,

Roger Hawkins played drums and percussion and Jimmy Johnson played guitar on "Killin' Time". The rest of the album tracks were recorded at several different studios across America and overseas.

The studio album did very well for Cat Stevens on both sides of the Atlantic, going gold in both the USA and Canada. The album also obtained a silver plaque in England for over sixty thousand copies sold according to the BPI.

30

MILLIE JACKSON AT MUSCLE SHOALS SOUND STUDIO

Artist Millie Jackson benefited greatly from the support of the Muscle Shoals Rhythm Section on her Spring Records albums and singles. She had three gold-certified albums, all of them recorded at Muscle Shoals Studio.

Mildred Virginia Jackson was born in Thomson, Georgia, in 1944. Like several other singers in the Muscle Shoals story, she came from a family of sharecroppers. Her mother died when she was young, so she grew up with her father. As a teenager she moved to New York to live with an aunt and started modelling for magazines. At the age of twenty, she started performing, developing an act that involved more talking than singing. Millie enjoying writing poetry and her songs often contained long spoken sections.

She signed for MGM Records in 1970, but soon left to join Spring Records, where she worked with Raeford Gerald. By 1971 she had her first hit, "A Child of God (It's Hard to Believe)", which reached number twenty-two on the R&B chart. The follow-up singles, "Ask Me What You Want" and "My Man, A Sweet Man", also sold well. Over the next couple of years, she released a series of R&B songs which established her success.

In 1974, Millie Jackson came to Muscle Shoals to record her fourth studio album "Caught Up", with Brad Shapiro as producer. It gave her the first gold album. The personnel on the album were: Millie Jackson (vocals, concept), Barry Beckett (keyboards), Roger Hawkins (drums), David Hood (bass), Jimmy Johnson and Pete Carr (guitars), Mike Lewis (orchestration), Tom Roady and Brad Shapiro (percussion). The album reached number twenty-one on the Pop album chart and number four on the R&B chart. The single taken from the album was "(If Loving You Is Wrong) I Don't Want to Be Right", written by Stax songwriters Carl Hampton, Homer Banks and Raymond Jakson. Stax artist Luther Ingram had recorded the song and sold over a million copies. Now the song helped Millie strike gold, attracting two Grammy nominations along the way. The next album "Still Caught Up" was less successful, but it features an excellent version of "Loving Arms", which was released as a single. Millie Jackson shared production duties with Brad Shapiro, and there are some strong backing vocals form Rhodes, Chalmers, Rhodes and Janie Fricke.

Millie Jackson in 2012 at the Howard Theatre, Washington

Photo: Polyester-queen (Wikimedia commons)

The "Feelin' Bitchy" album was released in 1977 and was her second album to be certified gold by the RIAA. This time the album project was recorded at several recording studios in America which included Muscle Shoals Studio, featuring

David Hood on bass, Rodger Hawkins on drums, Barry Beckett on keyboards and finally Jimmy Johnson on guitar. It reached number thirty-four on the Billboard Pop album chart and number four on the Billboard Top Soul Albums chart.

The final studio album to receive a gold plaque for Miss Jackson was "Get It Out' Cha System" in 1978 at the height of the disco era. It didn't quite hit the heights of the first two gold albums, but nevertheless Millie Jackson was the only female artist to obtain three gold albums based mainly on the Muscle Shoals signature sound. She recorded over a dozen albums for the Spring Records label, most of them with the Muscle Shoals session men, with regular chart entries. The Swampers must have enjoyed playing some R&B again!

Millie Jackson's Kent Records album

(used with permission of Ace Records)

Recommended Track:

1974 Millie Jackson: "(If Loving You Is Wrong) I Don't Want to Be Right"

31

MUSCLE SHOALS SOUND INTO THE EIGHTIES AND BEYOND: GOSPEL, COUNTRY AND ROCK

In the second half of the seventies, singer **Mary MacGregor** received a signature touch at the Muscle Shoals Sound Studio. She scored a big hit with the album title track "Torn Between Two Lovers" which was co-produced by Barry Beckett and Peter Yarrow (of Peter, Paul & Mary fame), with music support from the Muscle Shoals Rhythm Section. The song made it to number one on the Billboard Hot 100 Singles Chart week-ending February 5th 1977 (2 weeks) and to number one on the Billboard Adult Contemporary Singles Chart week-ending December 25th 1976 (2 weeks). The song also reached number one in Canada on the Canadian RPM Magazine Top Singles Chart listing week-ending February 26th 1977 (1 week).

In 1978, the Swampers decided that their studio was too small and moved into bigger premises on Alabama Avenue in Sheffield. Since 1969, they had played on over two hundred albums, helping to create over seventy-five gold and platinum records, as well as hundreds of hit songs.

The new building

Photo: Carol M. Highsmith 1920 (Wikimedia Commons)

During 1978 and 1979, **Dr. Hook** recorded a number of songs at the new Muscle Shoals studio, the best-known of which is "When You're In Love With a Beautiful Woman".

The final studio album of significance to come out of Muscle Shoals Studio at the end of the 1970s was "Slow Train Coming", featuring the classic hit single "Gotta Serve Somebody", by **Bob Dylan**. The album was co-produced by Jerry Wexler and Barry Beckett. This was the nineteenth studio album by the American singer-songwriter Bob Dylan, released on August 20th 1979 by Columbia Records. It was the artist's first effort since becoming a born-again Christian, and all of the songs expressed his strong personal faith in God. The album was the only studio project relating to the Christian and Gospel music sector in America to be certified platinum according to the RIAA.

The album became Bob Dylan's highest-charting album since 1976 by going to number three on the Billboard Top 200 Albums Chart in America. In England it went one position higher to number two on the UK Official Pop Albums Chart week-ending September 8th 1979. The album received a gold plaque from the BPI for over one hundred thousand copies sold across the UK. The album also received double-platinum status in Canada. On the Australian Kent Music Report Albums Chart the album went to number one week-ending October 8th 1979 for two weeks. The song "Gotta Serve Somebody" was awarded a Grammy Award for "Best Rock Vocal Performance, Male" in 1980.

In 1980 Dylan went to the Muscle Shoals Sound Studio to record his follow-up Gospel album, entitled "Saved". It was co-produced by Jerry Wexler with additional support from Spooner Oldham on keyboards and Tim Drummond on bass guitar. Drummond is well-known for playing with Eric Clapton, Miles Davis, James Brown, and Neil Young. The album "Saved" did not chart very well in the United States, but was more successful in England, receiving a silver disc from the

BPI for sixty thousand copies sold and peaking at number three on the UK Official Pop Albums Chart week-ending June 28th 1980.

Julian Lennon, son of the late John Lennon, experienced great success with his debut album released on Charisma Records in 1984. A portion of the album was recorded at the Muscle Shoals Studio with Barry Beckett and the Muscle Shoals Rhythm Section providing the music and arrangements. On January 9th 1985, the album was certified gold by the RIAA and then platinum on March 13th of that year for having shipped one million copies in the United States. Julian Lennon received a nomination for "Best New Artist "at the 28th Grammy Awards. The album also received a silver disc from the BPI in the UK.

Country groups also scored big with the support of the Muscle Shoals Rhythm Section. The first studio album by the Country music band **Oak Ridge Boys** was recorded at both FAME Recording Studios and Muscle Shoals Sound Studios in 1981 and released on February 10th 1982. The Muscle Shoals Horn Section, consisting of Harrison Calloway on trumpet, Ronnie Eades on baritone saxophone, Charles Rose on trombone and finally Harvey Thompson on tenor and alto saxophones, was used extensively on many tracks on the "Bobbie Sue" gold-certified album.

The entire project was a tremendous success for the group with its title song going all the way to number one on the Billboard Country Singles Chart week-ending April 3rd 1982 and reaching number twelve on the Billboard Hot 100 Singles Chart. Another single was released from the album entitled "I Wish You Could Have Turned My Head (And Left My Heart Alone)" which made it to number two on the Billboard Country Singles Chart. The album also reached the number one position on the Billboard Top Country Albums Chart week-ending March 27th 1982 (2 weeks).

The group repeated the same success with their next studio album "American Made" with support from the session musicians at Muscle Shoals Sound Studio and with additional support from The Nashville Hornworks.

The eighth country studio album by The Oak Ridge Boys, which was released in 1983 on MCA Records, featured yet another "crossover hit" with the song "American Made", which made it to number one on the Billboard Hot Country Singles Chart week-ending April 23rd 1983. The Oak Ridge Boys released a second single from the album that peaked at number one on the Billboard Hot Country Singles Chart week-ending August 20th 1983 (1 week) and at number one on the Canadian RPM Country Tracks Chart week-ending August 20th 1983 (1 week). "Love Song" was The Oak Ridge Boys' eighth number one Country Music single. The single went to number one for one week and spent a total of twelve weeks on the Billboard Hot Country Singles Chart.

During the early 1980s **Glenn Frey**, a solo male artist from the super Soft Rock group the Eagles, benefited greatly from working at Muscle Shoals Sound Studio with a series of hit albums to his credit. The first studio album was "No Fun Aloud", released in May 1982 on the Asylum label in the United States and the UK and soon gold-certified in America. His second solo album, just like first, was recorded at several studios with some tracks recorded at Muscle Shoals Sound Studio with David Hood on bass guitar and Barry Beckett on piano and synthesizer. This time the album charted higher than the first studio album, reaching number twenty-two on the Billboard 200 Albums Chart. The album "The Allnighter" achieved gold status with the RIAA, which gave Glenn Frey his second gold album in succession as a solo artist since leaving the Eagles.

The Swampers continued to work successfully at the new studio until 1985, when they sold it to Tommy Couch's Malaco Records (based in Jackson, Mississippi), which used the

Sheffield studios for its own artists, including Johnnie Taylor, Bobby Bland, and Little Milton, alongside its own facility in Jackson. Malaco finally sold the Alabama Avenue site in 2005 to a film company, Cypress Moon Productions.

Another American Country music group of significance who benefited tremendously from the support of members of the Muscle Shoals Rhythm Section was **Sawyer Brown** who started their recording career with the self-titled album "Sawyer Brown", released by Capitol/Curb Records in 1984. It was not until 1987 that members of the Muscle Shoals Rhythm Section started to collaborate with the group by working on an entire album entitled "Somewhere in the Night". The album was the group's fourth studio album. The song "This Missin' You Heart of Mine" is the title of a song written by Mike Geiger and Woody Mullis, which was released as a single in November 1987 as the second single from the album "Somewhere in the Night". The song reached number one on the Billboard Hot Country Singles & Tracks Chart and also peaked at number one on the Canadian RPM Country Tracks Chart week-ending March 19th 1988 (1 week). As well as regular members of the Muscle Shoals Rhythm Section on the album, there were also the two members of the famous Memphis Horns Section, Andrew Love on saxophone and Wayne Jackson on trumpet, plus Jack Hole on trombone.

The group's next album also features two members of the Muscle Shoals Rhythm Section. It is called "The Dirt Road" and was released on January 6th 1992. The album only featured David Hood on bass guitar and Roger Hawkins on drums. The album became the first gold-certified recording project for Sawyer Brown. The album had two outstanding singles that made it to number one on two different singles charts. The first single was the album's title track "The Dirt Road" which peaked at the top position on the Canadian RPM Country Tracks Chart week-ending February 15th 1992. The second single entitled "Some Girls Do" was released on March 4th 1992 and reached the number one position on the

Billboard Hot Country Singles & Tracks Chart week-ending May 23rd 1992. The singles also peaked at number two in Canada during the same period.

The following year the group had further success with another gold-certified album by the name of "Outskirts of Town", the tenth studio album and the second studio album to receive a gold plaque from the RIAA. The album was released in 1993 on Curb Records. It produced four hit singles on the Billboard Country Music charts, "Thank God for You" (the band's third and final number one), "The Boys and Me" (number four), the title track (number forty) and finally "Hard to Say" which reached number five. The number one single "Thank God For You" was written by Mac McAnally and Mark Miller.

The **Black Keys**' sixth studio album entitled "Brothers" was recorded in 2009 at the old Muscle Shoals Sound Studio, co-produced by the group, Mark Neill and Danger Mouse. It was released on May 18th 2010 on Nonesuch Records. The album became the band's commercial breakthrough, as it sold over 73,000 copies in the United States in its first week and peaked at number three on the Billboard 200 Albums Chart listing, which was the group's best performance to that point. The album's lead single, "Tighten Up", the only track from the album produced by Danger Mouse, became their most successful single so far, spending 10 weeks at number one on the Billboard Alternative Songs Chart and becoming the group's first single on the Billboard Hot 100, peaking at number eighty-seven and later certified gold by the RIAA.

The second single, "Howlin' for You", was also certified gold. In April 2012, the album was certified platinum in America by the RIAA for shipping over one million copies. It also achieved multi-platinum status in Canada and received a gold plaque in the UK for over one hundred thousand copies sold. In 2011 the album won three Grammy Awards, after been nominated for five, at the 2011 Grammy Awards Ceremony. The biggest success for the group was winning the Grammy for "Best

Alternative Music Album". The single "Tighten Up" also won the award for "Best Rock Performance by a Duo or Group with Vocals" and was nominated for Best Rock Song. "Black Mud" was nominated for "Best Rock Instrumental Performance". The fifth nomination was for "Best Recording Package", which Michael Carney won for designing the album artwork.

*

The four members of the Muscle Shoals Rhythm Section who had founded the Muscle Shoals Sound Studio were inducted into the Alabama Music Hall of Fame in 1995, as "four of the finest studio musicians in the world", receiving the Lifework Award in 2008. They were also inducted into the Nashville-based Musicians Hall of Fame in 2008. They had appeared on more than five hundred recordings. The list of artists that they recorded with is probably the longest of any session band, but it is not only the number of singers. It is also the variety of styles and voices, across so many genres, that makes them stand out. Most of the most famous names are covered in this book, but there are many more: King Curtis, Otis Rush, Joe Cocker, J.J. Cale, Linda Ronstadt, Tony Joe White, Jimmy Cliff, the Dells, Canned Heat, Joe Simon, Jose Feliciano, Dorothy Moore, Dire Straits, Eric Clapton, and a host of others.

The original studio had become a shop selling professional audio equipment and then an appliance repair shop. It was abandoned in the late 1990s, before being renovated and re-opened as a museum and recording studio. It was used, as we have seen, by the Black Keys in 2009 to record their album "Brothers". Finally, in 2013, it was bought by the Muscle Shoals Music Foundation and restored to its former glory, opening as a tourist attraction in January 2017.

CONCLUSION

In 2013, a film called "Muscle Shoals" was shown at the Sundance Film Festival. It gives a fascinating insight into how the music of Muscle Shoals came into being, with the story of the music told by the people who made it. The director Greg Camalier has spoken of his motivation in creating the film:

"Muscle Shoals comes from the heart – not only the film but the entirety of the tale itself…".

And, of course, the music does too.

The story started in 1959 in Florence, in the rooms above a drugstore, with a makeshift studio. Around the same time, Stax Records and Motown Records were being founded in Memphis and Detroit. Rick Hall, Jim Stewart and Estelle Axton, and Berry Gordy all shared the same dream: they wanted to bring Black R&B music to the prominence it deserved. They all shared the same problems too. They had to create new studios and find capable session musicians. They had to seek out talented songwriters. And, they had to learn how to survive in the world of business. Rick Hall probably had the hardest job of all, making his dream real in North Alabama.

When he was forced out of the Florence enterprise by his two partners, he found a way to launch FAME on his own. He found a building that he could convert, some young musicians who were eager to make records and a trio of gifted songwriters. Most important of all, he found Arthur Alexander, without whom the phenomenon of Muscle Shoals would probably not have happened. The money that Hall earned from "You'd Better Move On" set the ball rolling, helping to create the new FAME Studios, then inspiring Quin Ivy to set up Norala, and finally giving the Swampers the opportunity to set up their own studio too.

What stands out in the story of FAME is Rick Hall's relentless determination to make good music, whilst never being afraid to bring in young, inexperienced singers and musicians. In a segregated society like North Alabama during the 1960s, it was a bold decision to employ young White session musicians to back young Black singers. It was only possible because Hall had the vision to see that it would work.

At first things moved slowly. Hall was relying on contacts with Nashville to build the studio's success. Then, the second important event took place. Percy Sledge arrived at Norala Studio and was introduced to Jerry Wexler by Rick Hall. Without that introduction, the studios in Muscle Shoals may have withered and died. With Wexler and Atlantic Records on the scene, the music blossomed. The studios and the session men who played in them became well-known.

When the sessions with Aretha Franklin were suddenly terminated by Wexler, Hall showed that he had learned how to survive. He switched to Chess Records and brought new faces to Muscle Shoals. He also signed Clarence Carter and Candi Staton to his FAME label and built their careers.

Twice in the first ten years of FAME, Hall had to survive the loss of key members of his studio session band. It wasn't a problem on either occasion. New blood was quickly brought in, and the work went on. The Swampers' decision to leave FAME and strike out on their own was a brave move, especially as they set up their studio just a few miles from FAME and Quinvy, as Norala was now called. They had an offer of support from Jerry Wexler to give them confidence and their reputation was good, of course, but it wasn't easy.

In 1969, Quin Ivy was attracting local singers to Quinvy, whilst relying on the continuing popularity of Percy Sledge to ensure the studio's financial viability. He remained focused on Soul and R&B. Things were changing however at FAME and at

Muscle Shoals Sound Studio. Changes in musical tastes always bring a challenge to those in the music industry, and now Soul and R&B were beginning to go out of fashion. The response from both studios was to widen the musical scope of their operations, inviting visitors from the worlds of Pop and Country. The FAME Gang and the Swampers were versatile and adept at bringing out the best in singers from a variety of genres, and both session bands coped easily with the new demands. Big hits emerged from all three of the Muscle Shoals studios, which sealed the area's reputation as a place of inspiration and success.

Quinvy and FAME also gained a reputation for welcoming new, young singers to their recording facilities. This gave these operations a different feel from their competitors such as Stax and Motown, where established artists recorded on a regular basis. With the exceptions of Clarence Carter, Candi Staton and Percy Sledge, the majority of the recording artists who visited only came once or twice, to record some singles or an album or two. There was a steady stream of new faces, which probably added to feeling of excitement and anticipation.

A key feature of all three of the Muscle Shoals studios was the quality of the production and sound engineering. Despite not always being at the forefront of recording technology, the men who organized the sessions and set up the studios were all extremely talented. Rick Hall had a knack of finding just the right sound for a particular artist, but he was always prepared to go the extra mile to make sure it was on the tape. He worked his visitors and the session musicians hard. Dan Penn, Spooner Oldham, and Jimmy Johnson learned a lot from him.

At Quinvy, Quin Ivy, Marlin Greene, and David Johnson ensured the quality of the output. At Muscle Shoals Sound, all four of the owner/musicians played a part in production. The teams at each of the studios were highly skilled and could work very quickly and effectively. The Swampers could discuss plans for a recording with visiting artists like Paul Simon or the Rolling Stones and produce the perfect version in one or two takes. It is no surprise that Jerry Wexler recognised their talents and their efficiency when he worked with them at all three studios.

So, what is special about the signature sound of Muscle Shoals? The Soul music of Muscle Shoals is not as intense as that produced in Memphis. It is softer and easy on the ear. The drums are solid, without being intrusive. The guitars are usually well-integrated into the mix, in the style of Steve Cropper. The keyboards are often the lead instrument, with some outstanding piano and organ from Spooner Oldham, Barry Beckett and Clayton Ivey. The haunting, church-like lines played by Spooner Oldham on a tiny red Farfisa organ are a trademark of the Muscle Shoals sound. The horns are often softer too. The Memphis Horns played on many of the FAME recordings, with Charles Chalmers' trombone evident on many others. Later, Rick Hall set up the Muscle Shoals Horns, who played on most of the later FAME hits. The horn sound is generally smoother than that used in Memphis. Backing vocals also feature strongly on many of the songs from all three studios.

A portable organ made by the Italian company Farfisa

(Photo courtesy of audiofanzine.com)

The more up-tempo R&B of Muscle Shoals often owes a debt to Sam & Dave and is led by Wilson Pickett. However, the predominant style of the songs recorded at the studios, particularly at FAME and Quinvy, is the ballad. The songwriters developed a liking for story ballads, of the kind that were popular in Nashville amongst the Country music fraternity. Penn, Oldham, Fritts, Greene, Jackson, Moore and others were all capable of turning their hands to a variety of styles and subjects, but the favourite topic was male/female relationships going wrong.

The tone was set from the very start, when Arthur Alexander brought his song "You'd Better Move On" to Rick Hall's first FAME Recording Studio. Over time, more detail was added to the stories and the hint of sadness got stronger, but so did the feeling of resilience and determination to move on to better things. Clarence Carter's "Patches" is the most iconic of the family tragedy stories, set in a farming community in Alabama. It has been covered by George Jones and others, in a Country music version, but Carter took it into different territory. The key difference is the voice. Jones sings it straight, Carter sings it "natural" and for him that means with feeling.

Remember Greg Camalier's words?

"Muscle Shoals comes from the heart – not only the film but the entirety of the tale itself…".

"Patches" gives us a real insight into Rick Hall's story too. It was Rick Hall who suggested the song to Carter, because he recognised the situation it described. Hall was determined to make music that would appeal to Black and White audiences, but he wanted "feeling", and Black voices could deliver that better than anyone else.

FAME Recording Studio 2010

Carol M. Highsmith; Library of Congress (Wikimedia Commons)

List of Recommended Tracks

Below is the list of recommended tracks in year order. Listening to them all gives a clear insight into the key features of the Muscle Shoals sound and an understanding of how the sound evolved over the years.

1961 Arthur Alexander: "You'd Better Move On"

1964 Jimmy Hughes: "Steal Away"

1964 The Tams: "What Kind of Fool (Do You Think I Am)"

1964 Joe Tex: "Hold What You've Got"

1965 Joe Tex: "I Want To (Do Everything For You)"

1965 Joe Simon: "Let's Do It Over"

1966 Percy Sledge: "When a Man Loves a Woman"

1966 Percy Sledge: "Love Me All The Way"

1967 Arthur Conley: "Sweet Soul Music"

1967 Aretha Franklin: "I Never Loved a Man (The Way I Love You)"

1967 Aretha Franklin: "Do Right Woman, Do Right Man"

1967 Laura Lee: "Wanted, Lover, No Experience Necessary"

1967 James & Bobby Purify: "So Many Reasons"

1967 Tony Borders: "What Kind of Spell"

1968 Bill Brandon: "Rainbow Road"

1968 Clarence Carter: "Looking For a Fox"

1968 Clarence Carter: "Slip Away"

1968 Clarence Carter: "Too Weak To Fight"

1968 Irma Thomas: "A Woman Will Do Wrong"

1968 Irma Thomas: "Good To Me"

1968 Maurice and Mac: "You Left the Water Running"

1968 Maurice and Mac: "Lean On Me"

1968 Etta James: "Tell Mama"

1968 Etta James: "I'd Rather Go Blind"

1968 Etta James: "Do Right Woman, Do Right Man"

1968 Mitty Collier: "Got To Get Away From It All"

1969 Candi Staton: "Never In Public"

1969 Percy Sledge: "Faithful and True"

1969 Percy Sledge: "True Love Travels On a Gravel Road"

1969 Solomon Burke: "Don't Wait Too Long"

1969 Solomon Burke: "Uptight Good Woman"

1969 Lou Johnson: "She Thinks I Still Care"

1969 R.B. Greaves: "Take a Letter, Maria"

1969 Lulu: "Sweep Around Your Own Back Door"

1970 Clarence Carter: "Patches"

1970 Candi Staton: "That's How Strong My Love Is"

1970 Candi Staton: "How Can I Put Out The Flame (When You Keep The Fire Burning)"

1970 Willie Hightower: "Walk A Mile In My Shoes"

1970 Willie Hightower: "Time Has Brought About A Change"

1971 Willie Hightower: "Back Road Into Town"

1971 Bettye Swann: "Victim Of A Foolish Heart"

1971 Wilson Pickett: "Fire and Water"

1971 Candi Staton: "What Would Become of Me"

1971 Doris Duke: "Since I Fell For You"

1971 Freddie North: "Raining on a Sunny Day"

1971 Freddie North: "Cuss the Wind"

1971 Bobby Womack: "That's The Way I Feel About Cha"

1971 Z.Z. Hill: "Faithful and True" (recorded 1969)

1971 The Rolling Stones: "Brown Sugar" (recorded 1969)

1971 The Rolling Stones: "You Gotta Move" (1969)

1971 The Staple Singers: "You've Got To Earn It"

1972 The Staple Singers: "I'll Take You There"

1972 Mel & Tim: "Starting All Over Again"

1972 Laura Lee: "It's All Wrong But It's Alright"

1972 Candi Staton: "In The Ghetto"

1972 Candi Staton: "The Thanks I Get For Loving You"

1972 Bettye Swann: "Today I Started Loving You Again"

1973 Johnnie Taylor: "I Believe In You (You Believe In Me)"

1974 Z.Z. Hill: "It Ain't Safe"

1974 Z.Z. Hill: "Am I Groovin' You

1974 Millie Jackson: "(If Loving You Is Wrong) I Don't Want to Be Right"

1975 Odia Coates: "Heaven and Hell"

1975 Odia Coates: "The Woman's Song"

1975 Odia Coates: "Don't Leave Me In the Morning

1977 Eddie Hinton: "Hard Luck Guy"

2007 Bettye LaVette: "I Still Want to Be Your Baby"

2010 Spencer Wiggins: "Cry To Me"

2010 Spencer Wiggins: "I Never Loved A Woman (The Way I Loved You)"

2011 James Carr: "Love Is a Beautiful Thing"

2013 James Govan: "I Shall Be Released"

2013 James Govan: "Way Over Yonder"

Industry Awards for MUSCLE SHOALS

GRAMMY AWARDS

Rick Hall received a Trustees Award in 2014

Grammy Hall of Fame Awards

Aretha Franklin for the studio album "I Never Loved A Man (The Way I Loved You)", inducted 2009

The Staples Singers' single "I'll Take You There", inducted 1999

The Staples Singer's single "Respect Yourself", inducted 2002

Percy Sledge's single "When A Man Loves A Woman", inducted 1999

BILLBOARD AWARD

Rick Hall for "Producer of The Year" in 1971 by Billboard Magazine

ROCK AND ROLL HALL OF FAME

Percy Sledge inducted into the class of 2005

The Staples Singers inducted into the class of 1999

Aretha Franklin inducted into the class of 1987

"The first woman inducted into the Rock & Roll Hall of Fame, Aretha Franklin was an artist of passion, sophistication and command, whose recordings remain anthems that defined soul music. Long live the Queen." (Rock and Roll Hall of Fame performers category)

MUSCLE SHOALS

Gold and Platinum Singles

Clarence Carter

"Slip Away". Pop number 6 and R&B number 2, 1968
Atlantic 2508

"Too Weak To Fight". Pop number 13 and R&B number 3,
1968: Atlantic 2569

"Patches". Pop number 4, R&B number 2, and UK Pop
number 2, 1970: Atlantic 2748

Aretha Franklin

"I Never Loved A Man (The Way I Love You)". Pop number
9, R&B number 1, March 25th, 1967 (7 weeks) and UK Pop
number 36, 1967: Atlantic 2386.

Percy Sledge

"When A Man Loves A Woman". Pop number 1, May 28th,
1966 (2 weeks), R&B number 1, May 1st, 1966 (4 weeks),
UK Pop number 4, 1966 and UK Pop number 2, 1987:
Atlantic 2326

The Staple Singers

"I'll Take You There". Pop number 1, June 3rd, 1972 (1 week), R&B number 1, May 6th, 1972 (2 weeks) and UK Pop number 30, 1972: Stax 00125

Luther Ingram

"(If Loving You Is Wrong) I Don't Want To Be Right." Pop number 3 and R&B number 1, July 8th, 1972 (4 weeks): Koko 2111

Johnnie Taylor

"I Believe In You (You Believe In Me)". Pop number 11 and R&B number 1, July 21st, 1973 (2 weeks): Stax 0161

Arthur Conley

"Sweet Soul Music". Pop number 2, May 13th, 1967 (1 week), R&B number 2 and UK Pop number 7,1967: Atco 6463

R . B. Greaves

"Take A Letter, Maria". Pop number 2, November 22nd, 1969 (1 week): Atco 6714

Wilson Pickett

"Don't Knock My Love (Part 1)". Pop number 13 and R&B number 1, June 26th, 1971 (1 week): Atlantic 2797

Paul Anka with **Odia Coates**

"(You're) Having My Baby". Pop number 1, August 24th, 1974 (3 weeks): United Artists 454

Joe Tex

"I Want To (Do Everything For You)". Pop number 23 and R&B number 1, October 9th, 1965 (3 weeks): Dial 4016

"Hold What You've Got". Pop number 5 and R&B number 2, 1964: Dial

James & Bobby Purify.

"I'm Your Puppet". Pop number 6, 1966: Bell

Aretha Franklin

"I Never Loved A Man (The Way I Love You)": Pop number 2 1967, Gold certification on Atlantic Records. The album was partly recorded at FAME Studios, with the remaining tracks produced and recorded at Atlantic Recording Studios.

The Osmonds

"Osmonds": Pop number 14, 1970, Gold certification, MGM Records SE-4724.

"Homemade": Pop number 22, 1971, Gold certification, MGM Records SE-4770.

"Phase III": Pop number 10, 1971 Gold certification, MGM Records SE-4796.

The album was partly produced by Rick Hall at FAME Studios.

Donny Osmond

"The Donny Osmond Album": Pop number 13, Gold certified 13th December 1971: MGM Records

"Portrait Of Donny": Pop number 6, 1972, Gold certification, MGM Records. The album was partly produced by Rick Hall at FAME Studios.

"My Best To You": Pop number 29, Gold certification, MGM/Kolob SE-4872

Millie Jackson.

"Caught Up". Pop number 21, 1972: Spring 6703

"Feelin' Bitchy". Pop number 34, 1977: Spring 6715

Paul Anka

"Anka": Pop number 9, 28th September 1974, Gold certification, FAME Records/United Artist Records 314

"Time Of Your Life": Pop number 22, 17th January 1976, Gold certification, FAME Records/United Artist records 569

Mac Davis

"Baby Don't Get hooked On Me": Pop number 11, 30th September 1972, Platinum certification, Columbia Records 31770

"Stop And Smell The Roses": Pop number 13, 10th August 1974, Gold certification, Columbia Records 32582

"All The love In The World": Pop number 21, 8th March 1975, Gold certification, Columbia Records 32927

Paul Simon

"There Goes Rhymin' Simon": Pop number 4, 9th June 1973, Platinum certification, Columbia Records 32280

"Still Crazy After All These Years": Pop number 2, 1st November 1975, Platinum certification, Columbia Records 33540

Art Garfunkel

"Breakaway": Pop number 7, 11th January 1975, Platinum certification, Columbia Records 33700

"Watermark": Pop number 19, 11th February 1978, Gold certification, Columbia 34975

Johnnie Taylor

"Eargasm": Pop number 5, 27th March 1976, Gold certification, Columbia 33951

Rod Stewart

"Atlantic Crossing": Pop number 1, 30th August 1975 (4 weeks) and 11th October 1975 (1 week), Gold certification, Warner Bros Records 2875

"A Night On The Town": Pop number 2, 31st July 1976, Multi-Platinum certification, Warner Bros 2938

Rolling Stones

"Sticky Fingers": Pop number 1, 15th May 1971(4 weeks), Gold certification, Rolling Stones Records 59100 (partially recorded at FAME)

Cat Stevens

"Izitso": Pop number 7, 28th May 1977, Gold certification, A&M Records 4702 (partially recorded at FAME)

Bob Seger

"Beautiful Loser": Pop number 131, 1975, Multi-Platinum certification, Capitol Records

Bob Seger & The Silver Bullet Band

"Night Moves": Pop number 8, 8th January 1977, Multi-Platinum certification, Capitol Records 11557

"Stranger in Town": Pop number 4, 6th March 1978, Multi-Platinum certification, Capitol Records 11698

"Against The Wind": Pop number 1 (6 weeks), 15th March 1980, Multi-Platinum certification, Capitol Records 12182

"The Distance": Pop number 5, 15th January 1983, Platinum certification, Capitol Records 12254

Bob Dylan

"Slow Train Coming": Pop number 3, 15th September 1979, Platinum certification, Columbia Records 36120

Julian Lennon

"Valotte": Pop number 17, 24th November 1984, Gold certification, Atlantic Records 80184

Traffic

"Shoot Out at the Fantasy Factory": Pop number 6, 17th February 1973, Gold certification, Island Records 9323

Oak Ridge Boys

"Bobbie Sue": Pop number 20, 6th March 1982, Gold certification, MCA Records 5294

"American Made": Pop number 51, 1983, Gold certification, MCA Records

Glenn Frey

"No Fun Aloud": Pop number 32, 24th July 1982, Gold certification, Asylum Records 60129

"The Allnighter": Pop number 22, 25th August 1984, Gold certification, MCA Records 5501

Sawyer Brown

"The Dirt Road": Pop number 68, 1992, Gold certification, Curb/Capitol Records.

"Outskirts of Town": Pop number 81, 1993, Gold certification, Curb Records

The Black Keys

"Brothers": Pop number 3, 2010, Platinum certification, Nonesuch Records

About the Author

Kevin Tomlin has been studying music with a signature sound for over thirty years, with particular emphasis on Soul and R&B music originating from America, especially music from America's inner cities and urban areas such as New Orleans, Chicago, Memphis, Muscle Shoals, Detroit, and Philadelphia. His journey has uncovered the distinctive sounds that emerged from each location and gave each one its signature sound.

Kevin started his journey from personal experiences living in Jamaica from the early 1970s until 1979, when Disco ruled the charts. He was listening to music coming out of America via radio and seeing performances on television and at live concerts at the music theatre at college and at other live venues by many great legends, during a time when black music made inroads into popular culture globally.

While he was living in America, he began teaching music history. He specialised in "Music of Black Origin" and "Visual Arts in South Florida, USA", through the "Arts in Education" programme.

During this period Kevin was involved in the creation of special training programmes and workshops for music teachers in South Florida schools and other settings, using music history as the foundation to build exciting programmes of study and support for education professionals.

Since his return to the UK in 2000, Kevin has worked on a series of research programmes, providing consultancy services for multi-media organisations, schools, recording artists, cultural and faith-based groups, and entertainment professionals, all within the framework of "arts and cultural history".

He was appointed music historian for the GMIA (Gospel Music Industry Alliance), concentrating on matters to do with "Heritage and Legacy". The GMIA is a music industry trade organisation based in London and is part of the UK Music scene. In 2015 Kevin was appointed a director of the Gospel Music Industry Alliance.

Kevin Tomlin

If you have enjoyed reading about the Icons of Muscle Shoals, you may like to read volumes one and two in the series called Icons of New Orleans and Icons of Memphis, available from Kindle and Amazon

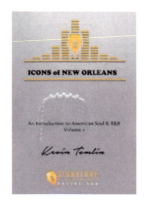

Printed in France by Amazon
Brétigny-sur-Orge, FR

20539720R10117